"Tertullian is certainly a significant early Christian voice. Yet despite (or perhaps because of!) his varied corpus of writings and many passionate opinions, there remain conundrums among scholars regarding Tertullian's actual views. In this brief study, Hannah Turrill addresses one of those areas: Tertullian's perception of marriage and sexual intimacy. From the cultural backgrounds and authors that informed his views, to the ways that his opinions may well have changed over time, this book adeptly surveys scholarship, reads Tertullian with alacrity, attends well to cultural and literary contexts, and makes insightful contributions to the ongoing scholarly conversation. A concise yet noteworthy book indeed!"

Megan DeVore
Professor of Church History and Early Christian Studies
Colorado Christian University

"Students of the Church Fathers usually find their writing on marriage and sexuality foreign and disagreeable. Tetullian of Carthage is a case in point. As Hannah Turrill notes, 'his views on marriage and sexuality are something of a conundrum.' Turrill's little book on Tertullian helps us to make sense of the conundrum by analyzing his writing on marriage and sexuality and locating his views in his ecclesial and social-cultural context. She shows us why we must read the Church Fathers in context and, in doing so, reminds us to consider the influence of our own ecclesial and social-cultural contexts."

David Robinson
Senior Pastor, Westminster Chapel, Toronto;
Adjunct Professor, Tyndale University

The Shameful Act

Studies in the Ancient Church

Early Christian Creeds & Hymns:
What the Earliest Christians Believed in Word and Song
Tony Costa

The Shameful Act:
Marriage and Sexual Intimacy in Tertullian of Carthage
Hannah Turrill

Roman Centurions:
A Historical Analysis of their Role in the New Testament
Steven A. Mercer

Christ Prays with Us:
Learning to Pray with the Early Church
Coleman M. Ford

The Shameful Act

Marriage and Sexual Intimacy
in Tertullian of Carthage

HANNAH TURRILL

H&E
ACADEMIC

The Shameful Act: Marriage and Sexual Intimacy in Tertullian of Carthage

Series: Studies in the Ancient Church

Copyright © 2022 Hannah Turrill

All rights reserved. This book may not be reproduced, in whole or in part, without written permission from the publishers.

Unless otherwise indicated, all Scripture quotations are from The ESV® Bible (The Holy Bible, English Standard Version®), copyright © 2001 by Crossway, a publishing ministry of Good News Publishers. Used by permission. All rights reserved.

H&E Academic, Peterborough, Ontario
www.hesedandemet.com

Cover design by Corey M.K. Hughes
Interior font: Equity Text A

Paperback ISBN: 978-1-77484-072-6
Ebook ISBN: 978-1-77484-073-3

Contents

Series Preface xi
Sex & the Church 1
   Michael A.G. Haykin

1. Roman Views of Sexuality & Marriage 11
2. Tertullian's Writings on Marriage & Sex 21
3. Tensions & Possible Solutions 43

Acknowledgements 55
Timeline of Tertullian's Works 57
Bibliography 59
Index 63
Scripture Index 67

Series Preface

Study of the Ancient Church was a common feature of Protestant theological reflection from the Reformation to the close of the long eighteenth century. Many of the Reformers, like John Calvin and Thomas Cranmer, were avid readers of extra-biblical, early Christian literature, as were most of the Puritans. They did not believe that this literature was canonical or on the same level as Holy Scripture, but they rightly recognized that the roots of the Reformed churches of Europe needed to be grounded in elements of Christian orthodoxy from the first five or six centuries of church history. Doctrinal convictions on the Trinity and the Incarnation that had been hammered out in those first centuries, for instance, still very much informed true Christian thinking. Moreover, Protestant claims to catholicity demanded recognition and evidence of continuity with the Ancient Church.

It is in the spirit of those Protestant and Evangelical forbears that these "Studies in the Ancient Church" are being published. Along with Calvin and Cranmer, Ussher and Owen, we recognize that early Christian thought has much to teach us. And in the various studies being published in this series, we listen afresh to those voices from the past, weighing what we hear against Scripture, discerning and cleaving to what is good and profitable for us in this day. These studies cover the entire range of the Ancient Church from the era of the so-called Apostolic Fathers down to the rise of Islam in the seventh century. We also include the occasional monograph on the New Testament texts, not because we consider the literature of that holy text to be on the same level as the literature that followed in the patristic era, but because the world of Roman Hellenism was a shared cultural context for both the New Testament period and the world of the Ancient Church.

It is the prayer of the publisher that this small academic series may, in its own small way, serve the cause of the Gospel and help advance the glory of God!

Sex & the Church

Michael Azad A.G. Haykin

Words not only bear distinct meanings but the way that they are employed reflects back on the cultures that coin them. So, for example, one evidence of the hyper-sexualized culture in which we live is the way that the term "sexy"—which used to have a distinct meaning of "sexually alluring"—has morphed into a variety of spheres where the adjective in years past would never have been used: course descriptions, cars, and cameras, for example, are all sexy—or not, as the case may be! This usage of this term even among Western Christians is surely indicative that the hyper-sexuality of our culture is re-shaping their world as well.[1] Of course, human sexuality is important—too important, in fact, to be misused in this way.

The Puritans on Sex and Marriage

Now, this overt sexualization of modern culture is, to some degree, a reaction against what is perceived to be Victorian prudishness, sometimes wrongly labelled as "Puritan," as we shall see.[2] More generally, it is a reaction against what is perceived to be the Christian view of sex. But what exactly is that view? To journey through the history of sex in Christianity is to discover a number of differing perspectives. There is the clear delight that Puritans like Richard Baxter (1615–1691) had in sexual intimacy within the context of marriage. Here is Baxter giving advice to married couples:

> "Husband and wife must take delight in the love, and company, and converse of each other." There is nothing that man's heart is so inordinately set upon as delight; and yet the lawful delight allowed them by God, they can turn into loathing and disdain. The delight which would entangle you in sin, and turn you from your duty and from God, is that which is forbidden you: but this is a delight that is helpful to you in your

---

[1] Witness further the adoption of the frankly absurd eisegesis of the Song of Songs that sees in the ancient text all kinds of sexual activities that titillate the modern palate. To read this book as primarily a "holy" sex manual surely misses key reasons why it is in the canon.

[2] As Marxist historian Christopher Hill once observed, "very few of the so-called 'Puritans' were 'Puritanical'" (*Intellectual Origins of the English Revolution Revisited* [Oxford: Clarendon Press, 1997], 260–261).

duty, and would keep you from sin. When husband and wife take pleasure in each other, it uniteth them in duty, it helpeth them with ease to do their work, and bear their burdens; and is not the least part of the comfort of the married state. "Rejoice with the wife of thy youth, as the loving hind and pleasant roe, let her breast satisfy thee at all times, and be thou ravished always with her love" [Proverbs 5:18-19].[3]

In a lifetime of studying Anglophone Puritanism and its worldview, J.I. Packer was convinced that the Puritans gave to marriage "such strength, substance, and solidity as to warrant the verdict that … under God … they were creators of the English Christian marriage."[4] Thomas Adams (fl.1612-1653), a renowned Puritan preacher in his day, argued: "There is no such fountain of comfort on earth, as marriage."[5] The Elizabethan Puritan author Robert Cleaver (fl.1570-1613) was of a similar mind: "There can be no greater society or company, than is between a man and his wife."[6] William Gouge (1578-1653), a leader among London Puritans and a key participant at the Westminster Assembly, emphasized that God intended marriage first and foremost for the mutual aid of husband and wife. "No such help," writes Gouge, "can man have from any other creature as from a wife; or a woman, as from an husband."[7] He encouraged married couples to engage in sexual intercourse with "delight, willingly, readily and cheerfully," since it was essential to marital companionship.[8] It may well have been Cleaver who came up with the following famous reflection upon the mode of Eve's creation: "The husband is … to understand, that as God created the woman, … so also he created her not of Adam's foot that she should be trodden down and despised, but he took her out of the rib, that she might walk jointly with him."[9]

---

[3] Richard Baxter, *Christian Directory* 2.7 in *The Practical Works of the Rev. Richard Baxter* (London: James Duncan, 1830), 4:122-123.

[4] J.I. Packer, "Marriage and Family in Puritan Thought" in his *A Quest for Godliness. The Puritan Vision of the Christian Life* (Wheaton, IL: Crossway Books, 1990), 259-260.

[5] Cited C. H. George and K. George, *The Protestant Mind of the English Reformation 1570-1640* (Princeton, NJ: Princeton University Press, 1961), 268.

[6] Cited Margo Todd, *Christian Humanism and the Puritan Social Order* (Cambridge: Cambridge University Press, 1987), 100. For further discussion, see Daniel Doriani, "The Puritans, Sex, and Pleasure," *Westminster Theological Journal* 53 (1991): 128-129; Leland Ryken, *Worldly Saints: The Puritans As They Really Were* (Grand Rapids, MI: Zondervan Publishing House, 1986), 41-42.

[7] Cited Edmund Leites, "The Duty to Desire: Love, Friendship, and Sexuality in Some Puritan Theories of Marriage," *Journal of Social History* 15 (1981-1982): 387.

[8] William Gouge, *Of Domesticall Duties*, 3rd ed. (London: Edward Brewster, 1634), 224.

[9] Cited Todd, *Christian Humanism and the Puritan Social Order*, 113. Cf. the following comment of the medieval author, Bonaventure (1221-1274), which might a source for Cleaver's comment: "Man and woman, according to the nature and properties of their respective sexes, were so made that they might be united to one another and thus have rest and support in and through each other.

The Puritan poet, Edward Taylor (1642–1729), of Westfield, Connecticut, once told his wife that his passion for her was as "a golden ball of pure fire" and that their "conjugal love ought to exceed all other," excepting only their love for the Maker of marriage.[10] It was thus not fortuitous that when that quintessential Puritan text, *The Westminster Confession of Faith*, listed the reasons for marriage, companionship came first. "Marriage was ordained," we read in chapter 25.2, "for the mutual help of husband and wife, for the increase of mankind with a legitimate issue, and of the Church with an holy seed; and for preventing uncleanness."[11] As Packer has noted, Puritan preachers and authors are regularly to be "found pulling out the stops to proclaim the supreme blessing of togetherness in marriage," which surely entails, among other things, sexual intimacy.[12]

Marriage and Sex in the Reformation and the Middle Ages

This clear delight in marriage and human sexuality as good gifts from God had its roots in the Reformation. Thus, for instance, after the death of his wife Idelette in March of 1549, John Calvin (1509–1564) wrote to his fellow Reformer and close friend, Pierre Viret (1511–1571) to tell him: "I am deprived of my excellent life companion, who, if misfortune had come, would have been my willing companion not only in exile and sorrow, but even in death."[13] This simple statement from one of the central figures in the Reformation, who was normally very discreet about his personal feelings, is a doorway into Reformation thinking about marriage—its innate excellence, its importance as a place of Christian affection and friendship, its role as a school of sanctification. A vital influence on Puritan writings about marriage was the 1541 translation of a work by Heinrich Bullinger (1504–1575), which was entitled, in its English format, *The Christen State of Matrimonye*. By 1575, Bullinger's book had gone through nine printings or editions.[14]

Because, therefore, man and woman are joined to each other by a strong and singular bond, one sex was produced from another. Because that union gives man rest, the woman was taken from man while he slept. Because a man is a woman's strength and support, it is said that the woman was made from his bone. And because in all these things there is a certain equality in a shared society, the woman was taken not from any old bone, but from the man's rib and from his side." Cited Fabian Parmisano, "Love and Marriage in the Middle Ages—I," *New Blackfriars* 50, no. 591 (August 1969): 605.

[10] Cited Roland Mushat Frye, "The Teachings of Classical Puritanism on Conjugal Love," *Studies in the Renaissance* 2 (1955): 158.

[11] On the significance of the order of reasons given for the institution of marriage, see Packer, *Quest for Godliness*, 261–262. See also Todd, *Christian Humanism and the Puritan Social Order*, 99–100.

[12] Packer, *Quest for Godliness*, 262.

[13] Cited Richard Stauffer, *The Humanness of John Calvin*, trans. George H. Shriver (Nashville, TN: Abingdon Press, 1971), 45.

[14] Frye, "Teachings of Classical Puritanism on Conjugal Love," 149.

The sixteenth-century Reformation is often remembered as a rediscovery of the heart of the gospel and the way of salvation, but it was also a recovery of a biblical view of marriage and sex. The medieval Roman Catholic Church had affirmed the goodness of marriage but at the same time argued that celibacy was a much better option for those wanting to pursue a life of holiness and serve God vocationally.[15] In fact, at the Second Lateran Council (1139), legislation was passed that only those who were celibate were to be ordained. But it was precisely here that reality collided with theological legislation, for many of those who were technically celibate priests in the High and Late Middle Ages were not able to actually live chastely. As Calvin later noted: "virginity ... is an excellent gift; but it is given only to a few."[16] One of the major scandals of the late medieval church was thus the very household of the parish priest, who was celibate, but not chaste, his so-called "cook" or "housekeeper" actually serving as his concubine.[17]

Of course, there were voices in the medieval world who retained key elements of the biblical view of marriage and incorporated love into the purposes of marital intercourse. Among them was Thomas Aquinas (1225–1274), who, although he valued the state of virginity above marriage, stated:

> Between a man and a woman there seems to be the greatest friendship; for they are united not only in the act of intercourse, which even among the animals produces a certain sweet society, but also throughout the whole of domestic living. In sign of this it is said in Genesis, ii, that for the sake of his wife a man leaves "father and mother."[18]

As Fabian Parmisiano comments on this text: "'the greatest friendship' is postulated between husband and wife and it is quite definitely considered

---

[15] John Witte, Jr., *From Sacrament to Contract: Marriage, Religion and Law in the Western Tradition* (Louisville, KY: Westminster John Knox Press, 1997), 24–25.

[16] Cited J. Graham Miller, *Calvin's Wisdom. An Anthology Arranged Alphabetically by a Grateful Reader* (Edinburgh; Carlisle, PA: The Banner of Truth Trust, 1992), 206.

[17] Susan C. Karant-Nunn, "Reformation Society, Women and the Family" in Andrew Pettegree, ed., *The Reformation World* (London; New York, NY: Routledge, 2000), 437–438. For Calvin, the Roman Catholic requirement of the celibacy of its priests was thus a "diabolical system," "a modern tyranny—in sum, "a doctrine of devils" (cited Miller, *Calvin's Wisdom*, 206; and Scott Brown, *Family Reformation: The Legacy of Sola Scriptura in Calvin's Geneva* [Wake Forest, NC: Merchant Adventurers, 2009], 114).

[18] Cited Fabian Parmisano, "Love and Marriage in the Middle Ages—II," *New Blackfriars* 50, no. 592 (September 1969): 652.

to involve the love act and all the 'sweetness thereof.'"[19] And to those who said that the marital act entailed immoderate passion, Aquinas was quick to respond:

> Only when the limits of reason are exceeded is passion considered to be immoderate. But the delight experienced in the marriage act, although it be most intense quantitatively speaking, does not exceed the limits prefixed by reason.[20]

Sex and the Fathers

However, a central problem for most medieval authors about marriage was the very thing that Puritan authors like Baxter encouraged, namely, sexual intimacy. The early medieval author Bede (c.673-735) spoke for the general medieval tradition when he maintained that the apostolic injunction to pray always could not be fulfilled if one was married and engaging in sexually intimate acts.[21] Sex precluded a robust prayer life. Bede is rightly regarded as a conduit of patristic convictions and this area of thought is no exception. Jerome (c.345-420), for instance, who was responsible for the Latin translation of the Bible known as the Vulgate, vigorously defended the view that celibacy was a vastly superior state to marriage, more virtuous and more pleasing to God. Jerome was convinced that all of those who were closest to God in the Scriptures were celibate. Jerome argued the very point that Bede affirmed and passed on to the Middle Ages: sexual relations between spouses were a distinct obstacle to leading a life devoted to the pursuit of genuine spirituality.[22]

Augustine (354-430), the North African pastor-theologian who corresponded frequently with Jerome and whose thought provided the foundation for much of the thinking of the Middle Ages, similarly maintained that the individual who devotes himself or herself to Christ to live a celibate lifestyle is like the angels. He or she experiences a foretaste of heaven, for in heaven there is no marriage.[23] Why, then, did God ordain marriage? In Augustine's eyes, it was primarily for the procreation of children. Commenting on Genesis 2, Augustine was convinced that Eve would have been

---

[19] Parmisano, "Love and Marriage in the Middle Ages—II," 652.

[20] Cited Parmisano, "Love and Marriage in the Middle Ages—II," 656.

[21] Robert Obach, *The Catholic Church on Marital Intercourse From St. Paul to John Paul II* (Lanham, MD: Lexington Books, 2009), 55.

[22] J.N.D. Kelly, *Jerome: His Life, Writings, and Controversies* (New York, NY: Harper & Row, 1975), 183, 187.

[23] James A. Mohler, *Late Have I Loved You. An Interpretation of Saint Augustine on Human and Divine Relationships* (New York, NY: New City Press, 1991), 71.

no use to Adam if she had not been able to bear children. What, then, of the biblical idea, found in this very chapter of Genesis, that the woman was made to be a delightful companion to the man, a source of comfort and strength? And what of the man as this for the woman? These ideas receive scant attention in the theology of Augustine.[24] Augustine argued that God instituted marriage for basically three reasons: for the sake of fidelity, that is, the avoidance of illicit sex; for the purpose of procreation; and as a symbol of the unity of those who would inherit the heavenly Jerusalem.[25] As for marital sex, it was only good and pure if it was done with a view to procreation: "children ... are the only worthy fruit ... of sexual intercourse," as Augustine once put it.[26] When sexual intimacy within marriage is directed by passion and not by a desire for procreation, he regarded it as a venial sin.[27]

And yet, there are some surprises among the fourth-century Fathers when it comes to the matter of marriage and marital intercourse. For instance, when the Syriac monastic leader known to posterity as Macarius (fl.380–410) reflected upon the believer's experience of the Spirit, he compared it to the marital experience of a man and woman. Even as the "deep, conjugal love" between a man and woman leads them to leave father and mother and all other earthly loves, so "true fellowship with the Holy Spirit, the heavenly and loving Spirit" ultimately brings freedom from the loves of this age.[28] Around the same time the Cappadocian Asterius of Amasea (fl.370–405) preached a sermon on divorce. He stressed that "marriage exists for these two things, love and offspring."[29] The addition of love and its placement in first place is not without significance. Speaking to Christian men contemplating divorce, he asked:

> In marriage, O man, both soul and body are united, so that disposition is mingled with disposition, and flesh with flesh. How then, are

---

[24] Leites, "The Duty to Desire," 384.

[25] Mohler, *Late Have I Loved You*, 68. See also the summary of Augustine's position in Witte, Jr., *From Sacrament to Contract*, 21–22.

[26] Augustine, *The Good of Marriage* 1, trans. Charles T. Wilcox in *Saint Augustine: Treatises on Marriage and Other Subjects*, ed. Roy J. Deferrari (Washington, DC: Catholic University of America Press, 1955), 9.

[27] Augustine, *The Good of Marriage* 6–7.

[28] Macarius, *Homily* 4.15, trans. George A. Maloney, *Pseudo-Macarius: The Fifty Spiritual Homilies and the Great Letter*, The Classics of Western Spirituality (New York, NY; Mahwah, NJ: Paulist Press, 1992), 56–57, altered.

[29] Asterius of Amasea, *On Divorce*, trans. Galusha Anderson and Edgar Johnson Goodpseed, *Ancient Sermons for Modern Times* (New York, NY; Boston, MA; Chicago, IL: Pilgrim Press, 1904), 153.

you going to sever the bond of marriage without suffering? How can you withdraw from this union easily and without pain, after taking your sister and wife not as a servant of a few days, but as a partner for life, a sister by reason of her formation and creation—for you were both made of the same element of earth and of the same substance—and wife because of the conjugal union [διὰ τὴν ἕνωσιν τῆς συζυγίας], because of the law of marriage? ... I refer back to the utterance of Adam: "This is flesh of my flesh and bone of my bones, this shall be called my wife" [Genesis 2:23].[30]

Yet, the dominant perspective on the divine purpose of marriage was that of Augustine—it was for procreation. And as such, it was a good thing.[31] In affirming this, Augustine was being guided by passages like 1 Timothy 4:1-4, which stressed that marriage is a good estate and one ordained of God. He was also the heir of the Church's battle in the second and third centuries with the Gnostics, who despised marriage and rejected it as a legitimate choice for one seeking to lead a spiritual life. In the words of one Gnostic, Saturninus (fl.100-120), "marriage and procreation are of Satan."[32] Clement of Alexandria (c.150-c.215) may well be citing Saturninus when he states his awareness of "those who say openly that marriage is fornication. They lay it down as a dogma that it was instituted by the devil."[33] Neither Augustine nor later medieval thinkers like Bede would have ever said such a thing, though they did believe celibacy was the doorway to a more spiritual life.

Now, this exaltation of the celibate state in the fourth and fifth centuries was tied intimately to the emergence of monasticism, which, in turn was a response to the growing nominalism in the post-Constantinian church. As Christianity became the government's preferred option, many were tempted to join the Church simply because it provided a way to get ahead in society. In other words, during the fourth and fifth centuries nominal believers entered the church in significantly large numbers to help bring about an identity crisis within the church. In essence that crisis can be boiled down to this question: "What does it mean to be a Christian in a 'Christian' society"? In the second and third centuries the lines between the Church and

---

[30] Asterius of Amasea, *On Divorce*, trans. Anderson and Goodpseed, *Ancient Sermons for Modern Times*, 139-140. For the Greek, see *Patrologia Graeca* 40.229A.

[31] Augustine, *The Good of Marriage* 9.

[32] Cited Irenaeus, *Against Heresies* 1.24.

[33] Clement of Alexandria, *Stromateis* 3.49.1, trans. John Ferguson in his translation of Clement of Alexandria, *Stromateis Books One to Three*, The Fathers of the Church, vol. 85 (Washington, DC: Catholic University of America Press, 1991), 286.

THE SHAMEFUL ACT

pagan society were fairly sharply drawn. But not so after Constantine. And the answer to this crisis that the Church came up with was the renewal movement that we call monasticism. In the long run this movement created as many problems as it set out to solve. As we have seen, one of these was an unbiblical exaltation of celibacy and denigration of marital intimacy.

Introducing Tertullian
Now it would be easy to regard these views of celibacy and sexuality as a product of the emergence of monasticism. Earlier Christian authors, though, had similar ideas. When Clement of Alexandria refuted Gnostic perspectives on marriage and sexuality in his *Miscellanies* (the *Stromateis*),[34] he pointedly argued that Christians are

> children of will, not of desire. If a man marries in order to have children he ought to practice self-control. He ought not to have a sexual desire even for his wife, to whom he has a duty to show Christian love. He ought to produce children by a reverent, disciplined act of will. We have learned not to pay attention to physical desires … In general, all the Apostle [Paul's] letters teach responsible self-control.[35]

And as this fine study by Hannah Turrill shows, the roots of the late patristic and medieval perspective on sexual expression within marriage are also evident in the writings of the eminent African theologian, Septimius Florens Tertullianus,[36] whom we know as Tertullian (fl.190–220). As a married man, it is not surprising that Tertullian was a fierce opponent of Gnosticism. And as such he penned one of the loveliest descriptions of Christian marriage in the literary corpus of the Ancient Church.

> How shall we ever be able adequately to describe the happiness of that marriage which the Church arranges, … upon which the

---

[34] It is fascinating that the Victorian translation of this work in the series entitled the *Ante-Nicene Christian Library*, which was published serially from 1867 to 1885, left the entirety of Book 3 in Latin. The other seven books of the *Miscellanies* were translated by William Wilson but Book 3 was clearly deemed too racy for the majority of Victorian eyes and was accessible only to those who were skilled in Latin! See *The Writings of Clement of Alexandria*, trans. William Wilson (Edinburgh: T. & T. Clark; London: Hamilton & Co.; Dublin: John Robertson & Co., 1869), 2:84–138.

[35] Clement of Alexandria, *Stromateis* 3.58.1-2; 3.86.1, trans. Ferguson in his translation of Clement of Alexandria, *Stromateis Books One to Three*, 292, 310.

[36] This is the name given to him by medieval manuscripts. See T.D. Barnes, *Tertullian: A Historical and Literary Study* (Oxford: Clarendon Press, 1971), 242.

blessing sets a seal, at which angels are present as witnesses, and to which the Father gives his consent? ... How beautiful, then, the marriage of two Christians, two who are one in hope, one in desire, one in the way of life they follow, one in the religion they practice. They are as brother and sister, both servants of the same Master. Nothing divides them, either in flesh or in spirit. They are, in very truth, two in one flesh; and where there is but one flesh there is also but one spirit. They pray together, they worship together, they fast together; instructing one another, encouraging one another, strengthening one another. Side by side they visit God's church and partake of God's Banquet; side by side they face difficulties and persecution, share their consolations. They have no secrets from one another; they never shun each other's company; they never bring sorrow to each other's hearts. Unembarrassed they visit the sick and assist the needy. They give alms without anxiety; ...they perform their daily exercises of piety without hindrance. ... Psalms and hymns they sing to one another, striving to see which one of them will chant more beautifully the praises of their Lord. Hearing and seeing this, Christ rejoices. To such as these he gives his peace.[37]

Building on the biblical given that marriage is a one-flesh union (Genesis 2:24; Matthew 19:4-6; 1 Corinthians 6:16-17), Tertullian here detailed what such a union entails with regard to Christian privileges and responsibilities. It is noteworthy that Tertullian assumed that a Christian marriage is one that takes place with the blessing of the Church, a perspective that can be traced back at least to Ignatius of Antioch at the beginning of the second century.[38]

As shall be seen in this study, though, there is more to Tertullian's view of marriage than this justly-famous text. I have long admired much about the works of Tertullian: his linguistic verve and convictions about the Triunity of God, his love of the Scriptures and courageous grasp of the basics of orthodoxy. Yet, it is evident that he had a prickly side and his embrace of Montanism exacerbated a strain of ethical legalism in his dealing with fellow believers. As the following pages reveal, his view of marriage was also not as rosy as the above quotation implies. And his view about sex

---

[37] Tertullian, *To His Wife* 2.8, trans. William P. LeSaint in *Treatises on Marriage and Remarriage: To His Wife, Exhortation to Chastity, Monogamy*, Ancient Christian Writers, vol. 13 (New York, NY: The Newman Press, 1951), 35–36.

[38] See Ignatius, *Letter to Polycarp* 5.

within marriage would have a long history in the life of the Church as this brief overview has made evident.

1
Roman Views of Sexuality & Marriage

There are two primary areas of historical context that are worthy of note for Tertullian's view of marriage. First, though some of Rome's own cultural commentators, such as Juvenal and Seneca highlighted what they viewed as appalling evidence of sexual libertinism and promiscuity in their society, Roman society, at least in the upper classes, did value sexual purity and held up monogamy as the ideal. This can be seen in the literary and legal sources. Second, there was, at least in the medical and philosophical communities, a movement that saw sex as potentially problematic for the ideal Roman man, advocating sexual moderation and restriction for a variety of mental and physical purposes.

Pudicitia and Sexual Purity in Literature

One essential element of Roman ideas of sexual ethics was the concept of *pudicitia*, or sexual purity or integrity. *Pudicita* was one of few terms in Latin that referred specifically and only to sexual purity and was essential to the honor of both men and women in Rome.[1] The virtue of men and women was partially determined by whether or not they were considered to possess *pudicitia* or sexual integrity.[2] The term was also an essential part of Roman sexual legislation under Augustus and Justinian, and assault on a person's *pudicitia* was viewed as an injury by law.[3] The legal importance of *pudicitia*, and therefore of its opposite, *impudicitia*, was not equal for all classes, however. It was most important for a free-born Roman citizen, only somewhat important for a freedperson, and non-existent for a slave,

---

[1] Rebecca Langlands, *Sexual Morality in Ancient Rome* (Cambridge: Cambridge University Press, 2006), 2. Langland's work was enormously helpful in this chapter's tracing of Roman attitudes to sexuality and marital intimacy in literature, as well as providing clues to primary sources to investigate.
[2] Langlands, *Sexual Morality*, 2.
[3] Langlands, *Sexual Morality*, 20–21.

as shown in the attestation of Seneca that "*Impudicitia* is a crime in the freeborn, a necessity in a slave, and a duty for the freed person."[4]

For married women, *pudicitia* was not merely a quality to be cultivated or a moral code to live by, but also, at least at one point, a goddess to be worshipped. The extinct cult of *pudicitia* was described by Livy, Propertius, and Juvenal as an example of the former commitment to sexual purity that they believed had been lost in the Rome of their day.[5] Though the nature of the cult itself is unclear from the extant evidence, Livy's account of the values of the cult reveals the values believed to be important for an upper-class married woman to cultivate. According to Livy's description in *History of Rome*, women could only participate in the cult of *Pudicitia* if they had manifest *pudicitia* (if they were "*spectatae pudicitiae matrona*") and if they had only been married to one man.[6] Though exactly how a woman would come to be considered manifestly *pudica* is somewhat unclear, the ideal of *pudicitia* being obvious to others displayed in Livy's description of the cult of *Pudicitia* is well attested.[7] The ideal of being married to only one man (a *univira*) expressed in Livy's description of the cult is also well attested in literature and on tombstones.[8] It is not clear exactly how these ideals were expressed or how many women actually exemplified these ideals, but that they were a part of the Roman understanding of an ideal wife is clear.

Displaying *pudicitia* for a woman seems to have been in some way related not only to a woman's activities in the bedroom, but also to the way she dressed and carried herself. In the second and third centuries, figures of the goddess *pudicitia* were frequently depicted veiling her face and a first century depiction of Claudia Quinta (who was believed to be a model of *pudicitia*) shows her with her hair covered, though her face is not veiled.[9] The significance of these depictions is unclear, but they do suggest a possible connection. Seneca also connects *pudicitia* and *impudicitia* with attire,

---

[4] Seneca, *Controversiae* 4. Preface. 10.
[5] Langlands, *Sexual Morality*, 57.
[6] Livy, *History of Rome* 10.23.9-10
[7] Langlands, *Sexual Morality*, 37.
[8] Marjorie Lightman and William Ziesel, "*Univira*: An Example of Continuity and Change in Roman Society," *Church History* 46, no. 1 (1977): 22.
[9] Langlands, *Sexual Morality*, 69-70.

as well as with conduct in public, saying that "A married woman who wants to be safe from the lust of the seducer must go out dressed up only so far as to avoid unkemptness. ... Let her guarantee her modesty [*pudicitia*] by denying her unchastity [*impudicitia*] with her look well in advance of her words."[10] He also observed that *impudicitia* was clearly revealed by dressing to attract attention and being forward in conversation.[11] In another place, Seneca clearly contrasted make-up, thin clothing and many ornaments with the display of *pudicitia* as an ornament.[12] These statements, alongside the material evidence, show that dress and deportment were deeply related to society's view of a woman's sexual integrity, though the bounds of dress and decorum are not entirely clear.

Though precise bounds of what constituted *pudicitia* and *impudicita* were somewhat hazy, its importance is clearly shown in the moral tales of Rome. One of the most significant examples of *pudicitia* for first century Romans, as well as Romans before and after, was the story of Lucretia. Her story is found throughout the literature of the first two centuries C.E. and beyond, including Cicero's *Republic*, Tertullian's *On Monogamy*, and Augustine's *The City of God*, but her story is most fully told in Livy's *Roman History*, which was written in the final decades of the first century B.C.E.[13] The story runs that Lucretia, the wife of Collatinus, was ravished by Sextus Tarquinius, the son of the king of Rome, after he threatened to kill her and place a naked, murdered slave next to her if she refused to acquiesce to his demands.[14] Rather than be suspected of such things, Lucretia allowed herself to be violated, but after she told her husband of the crimes of Tarquinius, which she considered to have taken her *pudicitia*, she killed herself, so that all would know that her adultery with Tarquinius had truly been by force and not by desire.[15] In order to preserve her good name, Lucretia allowed herself to be violated and her physical *pudicitia* to be lost, and then, to demonstrate her innocence and avoid being used as an excuse by women

---

[10] Seneca, *Controversiae* 2.7.3.
[11] Seneca, *Controversiae* 2.7.4; Langlands, *Sexual Morality*, 71-72.
[12] Seneca, *Dialogues* 12.16.4, cited in Langlands, *Sexual Morality*, 76.
[13] Cicero, *The Republic* 2.45-46; Tertullian, *On Monogamy* 17; Augustine, *The City of God* 1.19; Livy, *History of Rome* 1.57-58.
[14] Livy, *Roman History* 1.58
[15] Livy, *Roman History* 1.58.

who are truly unchaste (*impudica*), she killed herself.[16] Because of her commitment to purity, even to the point of killing herself, Lucretia was held up as an icon of *pudicitia* and an example for other women.[17]

The example of Lucretia reveals a great deal about the concept of *pudicitia* for an aristocratic woman in Rome. First, *pudicitia* is portrayed as something that can be clearly seen and is deeply tied to reputation, but also for that reason something nebulous and easily lost.[18] Before she is violated by Tarquinius, it is her evident chastity in behavior that leads him to desire her.[19] Rebecca Langlands observes in her book *Sexual Morality in Ancient Rome* that it was the praise of Lucretia's obvious *pudicitia* that eventually led to her downfall.[20] Lucretia's desire to maintain the appearance of *pudicita* ultimately forced her to endure both violation and suicide.

Also, the story reveals that *pudicitia* for women involved faithfulness to her spouse in both body and mind, but was destroyed if, for any reason, she engaged in sex with another man.[21] Once her body was violated, her *pudicitia* was irrevocably lost, and there was no way for Lucretia to prove her innocence and purity other than to die.[22] The lengths to which Lucretia was willing to go to defend her honor and her innocence, and the despair with which she met her fate reveals also the incredible importance of being seen and understood as a woman of *pudicitia*. Once that was stolen from her, she could not continue and, though she herself was blameless for the loss, she felt responsible to prove her own innocence.

For aristocratic men, the concept of *pudicitia* was more flexible than for women, but it was still very important for public perception. For men, moderation and restraint in sexual activities, rather than strict faithfulness was what defined *pudicitia*.[23] Langlands notes that having sex in itself was not wrong for an unmarried young man, so long as his sexual expression remained in the proper bounds, but his *pudicitia*, like that of a woman,

---

[16] Livy, *Roman History* 1.58; Langlands, *Sexual Morality*, 90, 95.
[17] Langlands, *Sexual Morality*, 94–96.
[18] Langlands, *Sexual Morality*, 37.
[19] Livy, *Roman History* 1.57.
[20] Langlands, *Sexual Morality*, 96.
[21] Langlands, *Sexual Morality*, 48; Livy, *Roman History* 1.58.
[22] Langlands, *Sexual Morality*, 94.
[23] Langlands, *Sexual Morality*, 134–135.

could be threatened or destroyed by improper conduct.[24] In Book 39 of Livy's *History of Rome*, he describes a young man named Aebutius, who was in a sexual relationship with a prostitute and former slave, but he specifically says that the relationship "in no way damaged his finances or his good name."[25] The main concern of the story, Langlands observes, is that the *pudicita* of Aebutius will be destroyed by his forced initiation into the cult of Bacchus.[26] Aebutius' career and prospects are only saved by his refusal to submit to the initiation, which eventually leads to a ban on the cult of Bacchus in Rome.[27] This story reveals that, though *pudicitia* was defined differently for a man than for a woman, maintaining sexual integrity of some kind was essential for the standing of a man in society.[28]

Though many of the sources that reference the concept of *pudicitia* are anecdotal and unclear about its boundaries, the seriousness with which the subject is addressed and guarded in both men and women is significant. The sources may not provide specific descriptions of what was and was not considered appropriate, but they clearly show that there was some level of cultural agreement that certain things were not appropriate for upper class and respectable people to participate in.

Sexual and Marital Legislation

The existence of ethical boundaries for sexual behavior in first-century Rome is further revealed in the marriage laws *lex Julia de maritandis ordinibus, lex Julia de adulteriis,* and *lex Papia-Poppea* instituted by Octavian Augustus in 18 and 9 B.C.E, which remained in place until the reign of Constantine. The marriage laws of Augustus specifically prescribed some sexual acts as *stuprum* or *adulteria*, for which a person could be tried in court.[29] Legally, sexual relations with any freeborn Roman woman other than one's own wife was a punishable offense, and those who abetted the offenders could also be punished.[30] A sexual act was considered *adulteria* if it

---

[24] Langlands, *Sexual Morality*, 115.
[25] Livy, *History of Rome* 39.9.
[26] Livy, *History of Rome* 39.9; Langlands, *Sexual Morality*, 115.
[27] Livy, *History of Rome* 39.19.
[28] Langlands, *Sexual Morality*, 120–121.
[29] Grubbs, *Law and Family*, 94.
[30] Langlands, *Sexual Morality*, 20.

involved a married woman and *stuprum* if it involved a widow or unmarried person of either gender, so long as the individual was a person of status.[31] Slaves and freed-persons, however, were not protected under this law. The punishments for commission of sexual offenses could be very severe, including property confiscation, exile, or even death, depending on the social status of the offender.[32] In addition to outlawing some forms of sexual expression, the Augustan marriage laws also regulated divorce (requiring husbands to divorce adulterous wives), and penalized unmarried and childless persons by limiting their ability to inherit.[33] Though the degree of enforcement of the Augustan laws is unclear and certainly depended on the region where the crime took place, the fact that these laws existed testifies to a value for sexual restraint outside of the context of marriage, at least when it came to men and women of status.

Sex and Health

In addition to the evidence of the legal and cultural value of sexual restraint, there is evidence that many Roman doctors in the early Empire also advocated for moderating the sexual impulses as a matter of health. The physician Soranus of Ephesus, in his book on gynecology, discussed a debate between the doctors of his day about whether or not a life of abstinence was a benefit or a detriment to health.[34] This discussion detailed an argument, with which Soranus ultimately agreed, that abstinence was ultimately a benefit to health in both men and women because both sexual desire and the emission of semen (which was believed to take place in both men and women) were believed harmful to a person's health, and because pregnancy and childbirth weakened women.[35] The primary argument against the health of abstinence was the belief that sexual intercourse eased the process of menstruation for women.[36] Soranus ultimately concluded

---

[31] Grubbs, *Law and Family*, 95.
[32] Grubbs, *Law and Family*, 95.
[33] Grubbs, *Law and Family*, 95.
[34] Soranus, *Gynecology* 1.30–32.
[35] Soranus, *Gynecology* 1.30.
[36] Soranus, *Gynecology* 1.31.

that even these concerns were unfounded and that, "permanent virginity is healthful, because intercourse is harmful in itself."[37]

Even the celebrated physician Galen, though he may not have believed intercourse was harmful in itself, argued that men in particular should use moderation in their sexual activity.[38] For Galen, as for many doctors of his day, the sperm was a carrier for *pneuma* and so emission of semen represented a loss of the vital spirit which he believed was the source of virility.[39] It was this loss of spirit, Galen argued, that resulted in feelings of tiredness after sex.[40] Because of the perceived risks of sexual activities, Galen and other doctors prescribed careful precautions surrounding sex for those who did choose to engage in it, and warned that those who did so without restraint must use extra care in their diet and exercise to ensure that they would not be adversely affected by their activities.[41] Galen did warn that sudden abstinence, especially in adolescents, could have adverse effects, but in most cases the use of sex was seen as something that should be done in moderation if done at all.[42]

Though medical opinions varied on whether any level of sexual activity was healthy, doctors in the early empire agreed that immoderate sexual activity was detrimental to health, especially for men. Taken on its own, this evidence does not speak to the actual behaviors of men in Rome, but it does indicate an atmosphere of concern about unrestricted sex and may suggest a movement on at least some level towards partial or even total abstinence from sex in the upper classes.[43] At very least, it can be concluded that attitudes towards sex were not always positive and that many were concerned about possible deleterious effects.

Sex and Philosophy
In addition to medical arguments about the possible ill effects of sexual intercourse on the body, there was also a strong philosophical argument for

---

[37] Soranus, *Gynecology* 1.32.
[38] Aline Rousselle, *Porneia: On Desire and the Body in Antiquity*, trans. Felicia Phesant (New York: Barnes & Noble, 1996), 12.
[39] Rousselle, *Porneia*, 14.
[40] Rousselle, *Porneia*, 14.
[41] Rousselle, *Porneia*, 18.
[42] Rousselle, *Porneia*, 19.
[43] Rousselle, *Porneia*, 19.

the moderation of sexual activities. Stoic and Platonic ideals of having every desire subject to reason were extended even into the realm of sexual expression in matrimony, where the object was rational control of the body.[44] It came to be believed that, in the words of Aline Rousselle, "Passion for another's body disturbed and obstructed reason and the freedom of the mind."[45] Lucan praised Cato by saying that he saw the purpose of marriage as only offspring, that he "even lawful love resisted," and that "no thought of selfish pleasure turned the scale in Cato's acts or swayed his upright soul."[46] Even when it came to acceptable behaviors, sexual restraint was seen as admirable because it displayed a command of reason over passion. Rebecca Langlands argues, in her book on sexual morality in Rome, that sex was seen as similar to food and drink, something that could be enjoyed, but with moderation, and that lust and avarice were seen as parallel vices.[47] Because logic was to hold sway in the mind of the ideal Roman, all areas in one's life, including sexuality, must be subject to restraint.

One Stoic philosopher who spoke especially strongly on the subject of sexual restraint was Musonius Rufus. Rufus believed that the only appropriate form of sex was that done in the context of marriage and for the sole purpose of procreation, saying that, "Men who are not wantons or immoral are bound to consider sexual intercourse justified only when it occurs in marriage and is indulged for the purpose of begetting children, since that is lawful, and unjust and unlawful when it is mere pleasure-seeking, even in marriage."[48] Any form of sexual expression outside of the confines of marriage and procreation, including those with prostitutes and slaves, which were widely accepted and not considered adultery, he prescribed completely as unlawful and immoral.[49] He argued that, though it was considered acceptable for a man to have a relationship with his own maid servant, it should not be done because it was seen as abhorrent for a woman to

---

[44] Paul Veyne, "The Roman Empire" in *A History of Private Life, Volume 1: From Pagan Rome to Byzantium*, trans. Arthur Goldhammer (Cambridge, MA.: The Belknap Press, 1987), 45–46.
[45] Rousselle, *Porneia*, 3.
[46] Lucan, *Pharsalia* 2.425–440.
[47] Langlands, *Sexual Morality*, 134–135.
[48] Musonius Rufus, *Miscellanies* 12.
[49] Rufus, *Miscellanies* 12.

do the same with a man servant, whether she be married or single.[50] It was nonsensical, he argued, to have higher expectations for a woman's ability to discipline her desires than for a man's ability to do the same.[51]

Double Standards
While the ideas of Musonius Rufus were undoubtedly more strict than even many other philosophers of his day, his writings, as well as those of Lucan and others, show a movement towards an ideal of sexual restraint within the educated upper class. Whether there was a similar current within the lower classes, or what their sexual ethic was is difficult to say because the vast majority of sources, like those listed above, come from members of the educated aristocracy. Both legal and literary sources, like the reference from Seneca quoted above, indicate that the sexual virtue of individuals of lower classes was not protected in the same way as that of those in the aristocracy, and that slaves were not permitted to legally marry until the second or third century, but beyond that, it is difficult to say.[52]

It is difficult to determine what may have been the differences in standards of sexual morality between the upper and lower classes, but the sources are clear that, at least in practice, there were differences between the standards for men and for women. As illustrated by Livy's narrative of Aebutius above, it was seen as perfectly acceptable for a man, especially a young man, to visit a prostitute, and doing so was not seen as a stain on his character or his sexual integrity.[53] Affairs with slaves were also generally seen as acceptable for men, and women could even be praised for ignoring and concealing their husband's affairs.[54] Adultery by the husband was primarily problematic if it occurred with a free-born woman. None of these things were seen as acceptable for women, as evidenced by the fact that Lucretia allowed herself to be raped rather than appear to have been caught in the act of sexual relations with a slave.[55] As discussed above, the medical

---

[50] Rufus, *Miscellanies* 12.
[51] Rufus, *Miscellanies* 12.
[52] Seneca, *Controversiae* 4. Preface, 10; Langlands, *Sexual Morality*, 20; Veyne, "The Roman Empire," 68.
[53] Langlands, *Sexual Morality*, 137.
[54] Langlands, *Sexual Morality*, 137.
[55] Livy, *Roman History* 1.57.

and philosophical discussions of the day, however, do bear witness to the fact that sexual restraint was viewed as significant for men, though their standards were different than those for women.

Concluding Thoughts

Though the Roman Empire has sometimes been depicted as a place of sexual profligacy and libertinism, evidence from a wide range of literary genres reveals both that a certain level of restraint was viewed as essential to one's status, and that there were medical and philosophical movements towards a much higher degree of restraint. At least for those in the upper classes, maintaining one's *pudicitia* was seen as a necessity, and for women that *pudicitia* was to be visibly displayed. Legal punishments restrained those who would seek to take advantage of women and children, so long as they were freeborn. Doctors generally advocated moderation in sexual behavior, and some supported complete abstinence. Philosophers as well argued for sexual restraint as evidence of the control of reason over one's life, and at least the Stoic Musonius Rufus advocated for sexual intimacy to be limited to procreation in the context of marriage. All of these trends bear witness to the fact that the Roman culture of the first two centuries did contain elements of sexual restraint, and that even total abstinence had its advocates. In general, the ideal seems to have been sexual faithfulness within marriage, though that looked different for men than for women. This background forms an essential element for understanding the view of Tertullian on marriage.

2
Tertullian's Writings on Marriage & Sex

A Sketch of Tertullian's Life

Tertullian of Carthage was a Christian philosopher-apologist in Roman North Africa in the late second and early third centuries C.E. His contribution is particularly significant in that he was the first major Christian writer to use Latin rather than Greek. Tertullian is also significant for his theological contributions in a number of areas, including trinitarian theology and the nature of the soul.

In trinitarian theology, Tertullian was the first to use the term "trinity" (Latin *trinitas*) to describe God, and to use the terms "person" (*persona*) and "nature" (*substantia*) to differentiate between the ways in which God is both one and three, in his treatise *Adversus Praxean* (*Against Praxeas*). This vocabulary was quickly accepted among Latin-speaking churches, and provided a basis for dialogue that was not present in the East, where heated controversies about the proper way to speak of the Godhead raged for another two hundred years.

In addition, Tertullian's work *De Anima* (*On the Soul*), was one of the first of its kind among Christians. In *De Anima*, Tertullian provided detailed discussion of the soul, including its origins and its nature. In contrast to his contemporary Origen, who believed that the soul was eternal, Tertullian suggested that the soul had a finite beginning, being created from the souls of the parents at the moment of conception, just as the body was. Though other theologians have since argued with Tertullian about the way in which the soul is created, his discussion of the soul as created at conception is significant in that it includes one of the first Christian arguments against the practice of abortion, making it a work of continuing relevance today.

Tertullian was also one of the primary Christian apologists to respond to the arguments of Marcion, an early heretic who suggested that the Father of Jesus Christ was not the same as the God of the Old Testament. Tertullian argued strongly against this view, affirming the goodness of creation and the consistency of God's character and actions throughout history.

Unlike many of the earliest apologists in the second and third centuries, Tertullian seems to have been a lay person with no official ecclesiastical role, though he did not hesitate to level sweeping critiques at behavior and leadership in the church in his day. He was deeply disturbed by what he viewed as the laxity of the church in general, and he strove to convince others of the necessity of spiritual rigor including frequent fasting and abstention from the typical entertainments of the day. He also firmly believed that the church must be pure, and because of this, that pardon for sin after baptism required significant penance and was sometimes impossible (as in the case of fornication).

The precise date of Tertullian's conversion to Christianity is not known, but he is thought to have become a believer as an adult. He was married and seems to have been fairly happy in his marriage, as evidenced by his extant writing *Ad Uxorum* (*To His Wife*), but little is known about his wife or the circumstances of his marriage, though it was likely before his conversion. Based on his style of writing, some have suggested that Tertullian may have had a legal career of some kind, but the evidence for this is scant and could be otherwise interpreted.[1]

Though Tertullian's writings were influential in a number of areas, he was viewed with suspicion by later church fathers because of his involvement with Montanism. Augustine included him (along with a somewhat mysterious group known as the *Tertullianistae*) in his listing of heretics because of his involvement with the Montanists (also called Cataphrygians) in the rejection of second marriage.[2] Tertullian's precise relationship with the group, and even the status of the group as part distinct from the orthodox church is debated. Some scholars, such as Geoffrey Dunn, have questioned whether Tertullian ever broke fully with the catholic community, or if Montanism was just a sect within the church at Carthage.[3] Despite the

---

[1] Eric Osborn, *Tertullian: First Theologian of the West* (Cambridge: Cambridge University Press, 1997), 8–9.

[2] Augustine, *De haeresibus ad Quodvultdeus* 86.

[3] Geoffery Dunn, *Tertullian* (New York:Routledge, 2004), 8–9.

presence of this debate, it generally acknowledged that Montanism played a significant role in Tertullian's life and thought.

Tertullian's writings are generally divided into three periods, related to his degree of involvement in Montanism: the period from roughly 198 to 206, when little to no Montanist influence is present; the period from 207 or 208 to 212, when his writings show distinct Montanist sympathies, but he still associated himself with the catholic church; and the final period of his life beginning in 213 until his death, which may be anywhere between the 220s to around 240, when he seems to have dissociated himself from what he called "carnal" (*psychichos*) Christianity (catholic Christianity) and may have converted to Montanism.[4] It is clear from his writings that Tertullian's thought underwent significant change and development throughout his life, and because of this, as Geoffrey Dunn observes, it is essential that any study of Tertullian's thought follow the chronology of his writings and acknowledge change and development.[5]

De Cultu Feminarum

The earliest of Tertullian's writings to touch on the issue of sexual intercourse or sexual desire is his *De Cultu Feminarum* or *On the Dress of Women*. The work contains two separate treatments of the issue of women's apparel, which were originally two separate works.[6] The portion relating to sex is found partway through the second of these books. The purpose of both books seems to have been to convince Christian women that they should no longer be concerned with their dress in the way that they were before they were converted.[7] In these works, he sharply critiqued undue elegance and luxury in dress, saying that these were inappropriate for believing women and stressing the importance of leaving pagan

---

[4] For this classification, see Osborn, *Tertullian*, 9. In contrast, Dunn sees the division of Tertullian's life into three distinct periods as problematic, and instead argues that his thought developed gradually over time in a Montanist direction, but always remained within the bounds of orthodoxy (*Tertullian*, 8-9).

[5] Dunn, *Tertullian*, 8-9.

[6] Rudolph Arbesmann, Emily Joseph Daly, and Edwin Quain, Introduction to "The Apparel of Women," by Tertullian, in *Tertullian: Disciplinary, Moral and Ascetical Works*, The Fathers of the Church 40 (New York: The Fathers of the Church, 1959), 111.

[7] Arbesmann, Daly, and Quain., Introduction to "The Apparel of Women," 111.

views for a total commitment to Christ.[8] Though the precise dates of the books are not known, it is clear that even the first book was written after his work *De Spectaculis*, since it makes explicit reference to that work, and both were likely written after *De Oratione*, since that work briefly touches on the subject of women's clothing, but without mentioning that another work on the subject had been written.[9] Since none of the aforementioned works show any evidence of Montanist sympathies at all, they have all been dated between 197 and 201, though some have suggested that *De Cultu* may have been written as late as 206.[10]

Tertullian began Book 2 of *De Cultu* by praising the virtue of modesty as playing a role in the salvation of men and women. He descried the abandonment of modesty of dress by women in his day, particularly among those women who continued to dress with all of the finery they did before they became believers.[11] He then exhorted his audience of believing women to be perfect as their heavenly Father is perfect, suggesting that modesty of dress was an essential element of this perfection.[12]

After this discussion of the importance of modesty, Tertullian turned to give a definition of modesty that hints at his views of sexual intercourse and sexual attraction. He wrote, "You must know that perfect modesty, that is Christian modesty, requires not only that you never desire to be an object of desire on the part of others, but that you even hate to be one."[13] Though Tertullian did not here give a full explanation of his views on sexual desire, the unqualified way in which he excluded a believing woman from wanting to be desired at any time, even urging her to hate the idea of being desired, suggests that his view of desire in general is quite negative. In his view, it seems, Christian woman should not only refrain from seeking sexual attention but should desire to avoid it under all circumstances.

---

[8] Arbesmann, Daly, and Quain, Introduction to "The Apparel of Women," 111, 115.

[9] Arbesmann, Daly, and Quain, Introduction to "The Apparel of Women," 115.

[10] Arbesmann, Daly, and Quain, Introduction to "The Apparel of Women," 115; Osborn, *Tertullian*, 9.

[11] Tertullian, *De Cultu Feminarum* 2.1.1–3, translated by Rudolph Arbesmann, Emily Joseph Daly, and Edwin Quinn in *Tertullian: Disciplinary, Moral and Ascetical Works*, The Fathers of the Church 40 (New York: The Fathers of the Church, 1959).

[12] Tertullian, *De Cultu Feminarum* 2.1.4.

[13] Tertullian, *De Cultu* 2.2.1.

Tertullian's view of the relationship of sexual desire and modesty is further clarified later in the treatise where he wrote,

> Why do we excite concupiscence in others? If the Lord in amplifying the Law does not make a distinction in penalty between the actual commission of fornication and its desire, I do not know whether He will grant impunity to one who is the cause of perdition to another. ... [E]ven though you are free from the actual crime of unchastity, you are not altogether free from the odium.[14]

In saying this, Tertullian referenced Jesus' words in Matthew 5:28 that connect looking at woman with lust and committing an act of adultery. The precise situation of which he was speaking is unclear, but his language does suggest that he saw at least unlawful sexual desire as so problematic that women who dressed so as to excite it were tainted by it, if not actually culpable.

Only in one short section of the work did Tertullian address these issues in the context of the responsibility of married women to their husbands. He wrote,

> If I were speaking to Gentiles, I would give you a Gentile precept and one that is common to all: you are bound to please no one except your own husbands. And you will please your husbands in the proportion that you take no pains to please anyone else. Be unconcerned, blessed sisters: no wife is really ugly to her own husband.[15]

Later, he further clarified this statement by writing, "Every husband demands that his wife be chaste; but beauty a Christian husband certainly does not demand, because we Christians are not fascinated by the same things that the Gentiles think to be good."[16]

While neither of these statements clearly indicate Tertullian's view of the propriety of sexual desire within the context of marriage, the evident unconcern for a wife's desire to make herself desirable to her husband suggests a view that was ambivalent at least. Tertullian was unequivocal that

---

[14] Tertullian, *De Cultu* 2.2.4
[15] Tertullian, *De Cultu* 2.4.1.
[16] Tertullian, *De Cultu* 2.4.2.

women should feel no obligation to please any man besides their husbands, citing the fact that even unbelieving women (Gentiles) were expected to please only their husbands. His language regarding the values of believers, however, suggests that the believing wife need not even seek to please her own husband because her beauty is not necessary to him because he "does not demand" it. This is further supported by the way he ended the section, querying, "For whose sake, then, are you cultivating your beauty? If for a Christian, he does not demand it. ... Why then are you eager to please ... one who does not desire it?"[17] For Tertullian, a believing woman ought not to be concerned with enhancing her physical beauty, even for her husband, and a believing husband ought not desire her to do so. Since Tertullian clearly connected physical beauty to sexual desire and affirmed that such beauty ought not to matter to a Christian, the question may be asked whether, according to Tertullian, any kind of sexual desire or desirability has a place in even a married Christian's life.

Ad Uxorem

Tertullian's most famous work on Christian marriage is his letter to his wife, which focuses primarily on the topic of remarriage after the death of a spouse. Though this letter, like the majority of Tertullian's writings, is difficult to date precisely, it is believed to have been written between 200 and 206, before Tertullian's turn towards Montanism, and the work bears little to no evidence of Montanist influence.[18] The first part of the letter is an attempt to convince his wife not to remarry after Tertullian's death, should he predecease her.[19] Following this first section is an impassioned plea that, if she did choose to remarry, she should not marry an unbeliever.[20] The letter ends with a heart-felt and beautiful description of the joys of a Christian marriage meant to dissuade his wife from considering marriage to an unbeliever.[21]

---

[17] Tertullain, *De Cultu* 2.4.2.

[18] William Le Saint, Introduction to "To His Wife," by Tertullian, in *Treatises on Marriage and Remarriage: To His Wife, Exhortation to Chastity, Monogamy*, Ancient Christian Writers 13 (New York: The Newman Press, 1951), 8.

[19] Le Saint, Introduction to "To His Wife," 5.

[20] Le Saint, Introduction to "To His Wife," 7.

[21] Tertullian, *Ad Uxorem*, 2.8, translated by William Le Saint, in *Treatises on Marriage and Remarriage: To His Wife, Exhortation to Chastity, Monogamy*, Ancient Christian Writers 13 (New

Though Tertullian's letter to his wife does include a moving depiction of the good of a Christian marriage near the end, Tertullian was clear in the first part of his letter that celibacy was superior to marriage for the Christian. He wrote,

> The Apostle ... teaches us what is better than this "good" [marriage] when he says that he permits marriage, but prefers celibacy. ... [M]arriage is conceded to us on the principle that we marry because we must. But what necessity proffers necessity cheapens. ... Marriage, forsooth, is better because burning is worse! But how much better it is neither to marry nor to burn.[22]

As David Hunter commented in his discussion of this passage, this makes marriage "merely a lesser evil than fornication."[23] Though these statements are not explicitly connected with sex, it is clear that Tertullian saw total chastity and celibacy as a significantly preferable state to marriage. It was for this reason that Tertullian advised his wife to remain a widow after his death.[24] Marriage, and with it any kind of sexual activity, becomes something merely allowed as the lesser of two evils.

In the second section the of the letter to his wife, Tertullian also argued that any marriage between a believer and an unbeliever amounted to fornication. He spent substantial time examining the commands of Paul regarding those who were already married when converted and arguing that there is a distinct difference between the situation of a person who is already married to a pagan when converted and that of a converted person who chooses to marry a pagan.[25] In the course of this discussion, he specifically addressed the statement of Paul in 1 Corinthians 7:13–15 that the flesh of the unbelieving spouse is sanctified because of the believer so that the children of the believer are not defiled.[26] Tertullian extended the logic of this passage to argue that the conversion of one spouse and the resulting sanctification of the unbelieving spouse also protects the believer from

---

York: The Newman Press, 1951).
[22] Tertullian, *Ad Uxorem* 1.3.
[23] Hunter, *Marriage*, 117.
[24] Tertullian, *Ad Uxorem* 1.3.
[25] Tertullian, *Ad Uxorem* 2.2.
[26] Tertullian, *Ad Uxorem* 2.2.

defilement by the other person, saying "Scripture states that those who are converted while living in marriage with a pagan are not defiled, because their partners are sanctified along with them."[27] When a believer married a pagan, however, the same exception did not apply because the conversion happened before the marriage and so did not sanctify the body of the unbelieving spouse.[28] Tertullian concluded by saying, "In light of all this it is evident that Christians who enter into marriage with pagans commit a sin of fornication and are to be cut off completely from communion with the brethren."[29] Tertullian's statements make clear that, even in the context of marriage, he saw sexual contact between Christians and pagans as amounting to sexual immorality, unless the marriage took place before the believing spouse was converted.

In the midst of his discussion of the evils of a mixed marriage of a Christian woman and a pagan man, Tertullian also gestured to the place of sex within a Christian marriage. He wrote that a woman in a mixed marriage, in addition to dressing to attract her husband's desire, which was unnecessary for the wife of a Christian, would "openly flaunt the sordid secrets of marital intimacies which, among Christians, are regarded as necessary functions of sex and performed with modesty and moderation, as under the eyes of God."[30] It is unclear to what kind of cultural trend he was referring when it came to pagans "openly flaunting" their sexual activities, but he did communicate a value for moderation in the practice of sex in Christian marriage. The reference to sex as merely "necessary" also lacks any kind of romanticism about the conjugal act. Aside from those few observations, his position on the value of sex within marriage is difficult to pinpoint, and there are no clear references to sexual relationship in Tertullian's description of the beauty of the Christian marriage.

Adversus Marcionem
Tertullian's work *Against Marcion*, or *Adversus Marcionem*, primarily counters Marcion's arguments that the God of the Old Testament is different

---

[27] Tertullian, *Ad Uxorem* 2.2.
[28] Tertullian, *Ad Uxorem* 2.2.
[29] Tertullian, *Ad Uxorem* 2.3.
[30] Tertullian, *Ad Uxorem* 2.3.

from the God of the New Testament and that Christ did not come in the flesh, as well as his extreme ascetic practices. The work went through several editions during Tertullian's life, the earliest of which may have been published as early as 198.[31] The edition that is extant contains some elements of Montanist theology, but gives no evidence of a rift between Tertullian and the "orthodox" party, so it has been dated to between 207 and 208.[32] *Adversus Marcionem* is particularly relevant to the present discussion because, in the context of an argument against the reality of Marcion's God, Tertullian addressed the Marcionite practice of abandoning marriage altogether, even to the point of annulling marriages between would-be converts.[33]

According to Tertullian's description, Marcion required all who would seek baptism to be virgins, celibate, or widows.[34] If a married person sought baptism, that individual would be required to divorce his or her spouse before he or she could be baptized.[35] In response to this, Tertullian affirmed that, though celibacy was better than marriage, marriage (and marital intercourse) was still good.[36] He wrote, "For we do not repudiate marital intercourse, but give it lower rank: nor do we demand chastity, but advise it, retaining both the good thing and the better, to be followed according to each man's powers."[37] He also stated that, even though Christians saw celibacy as superior to marriage, that did not mean that marriage was then rejected because God himself made and blessed marriage, saying, "He [the Creator], in consideration of the honor of that estate, blessed matrimony for the increase of mankind."[38]

With the goodness of marriage as created by God in view, Tertullian argued that marriage and sexual intimacy must not be taken as sinful merely because they could be misused, saying,

---

[31] Ernest Evans, Introduction to *Tertullian: Adversus Marcionem*, by Tertullian, (Oxford: Clarendon Press, 1972), xviii; Osborn, *Tertullian*, 9.

[32] Evans, Introduction to *Adversus*, xviii; Osborn, *Tertullian*, 9.

[33] Tertullian, *Adversus Marcionem* 1.28, translated by Ernest Evans, in *Tertullian: Adversus Marcionem*, by Tertullian (Oxford: Clarendon Press, 1972).

[34] Tertullian, *Adversus Marcionem* 1.28.

[35] Tertullian, *Adversus Marcionem* 1.29.

[36] Tertullian, *Adversus Marcionem* 1.29.

[37] Tertullian, *Adversus Marcionem* 1.29

[38] Tertullian, *Adversus Marcionem* 1.29.

> So then food need not be condemned, because when too curiously sought after it conduces to gluttony; neither is clothing to be called to account simply because, when bought at too high a price, it becomes proud and pretentious. So neither need marriage and it obligations be held in contempt just because, when unrestrained and uninhibited, it blazes out into wantonness. There is a wide difference between purpose and misuse, between moderation and excess.[39]

Though he did not explicitly mention sex here, the statement seems to suggest that marriage, and even moderate amounts of sex between married persons are appropriate, so long as they do not reach an excessive level. There is a place at which Tertullian believed that sexual behavior, even within marriage, might be inappropriate, but that did not mean that the entire institution was reprehensible.

In fact, Tertullian suggested that the legitimacy of sex within marriage was what made celibacy itself honorable.[40] He wrote,

> If there is to be no marital intercourse there is no chastity. Commendation given to abstinence is of no account when prohibition is imposed, since there are some things which obtain approval by contrast. Just as strength is made perfect in weakness, so does abstinence from intercourse become remarkable while intercourse is allowed.[41]

According to this logic, if sex within marriage was illegitimate, there would be nothing at all meritorious in celibacy. It is only because marital intimacy is an allowable option that choosing celibacy deserves special honor. This argument makes it clear that, though Tertullian saw celibacy as superior to marriage, he did believe that marriage was good and allowed for the Christian.

Though Tertullian did not talk in detail about what kinds of sexual activity within marriage are acceptable, the legitimacy of marital intimacy in service of procreation is made clear in Tertullian's statements at the end

---

[39] Tertullian, *Adversus Marcionem* 1.29.
[40] Tertullian, *Adversus Marcionem* 1.29.
[41] Tertullian, *Adversus Marcionem* 1.29.

of the section, where he berated Marcion and his supposed God for hating that practice which is the origin of all men. He wrote,

> How can he desire the salvation of the man whom he forbids to be born, as he does by abolishing the act from which birth arises? How can he have one on whom to set the seal of his goodness, when he does not suffer such to exist? How can he show affection to one of whose origin he does not approve?[42]

If Marcion's God saw all sexual intimacy as illegitimate, Tertullian argued, how could he love any individual person, because all people are born from a sexual act? Tertullian here clearly suggested that at least procreation is a legitimate use of sex within the context of marriage. For him, if God is to love people, who are born of marriage, marriage and procreation must be themselves good. Tertullian did not, however, specifically address the legitimacy of marital intimacy outside of the demands of procreation.

De Exhortatione Castitatis

The work that most specifically addresses the issue of sexual intimacy within marriage is Tertullian's *De Exhortatione Castitatis* or *Exhortation to Chastity*. This treatise was likely written sometime between 204-212, when Tertullian was beginning to be interested in Montanist ideas but had not yet separated himself from the rest of Christian society.[43] In this treatise, he positively references teaching of the Montanist prophetess Prisca, but he nowhere speaks negatively of the teaching of the church.[44] The intent of the treatise was to discourage a male friend or acquaintance of Tertullian's from remarrying after the death of his wife.[45] This treatise is particularly interesting because, though it follows a very similar argument to his previous work directed to his wife, the view of marriage he presents

---

[42] Tertullian, *Adversus Marcionem* 1.29.
[43] William P. Le Saint, Introduction to *Exhortation to Chastity*, by Tertullian, in *Treatises on Marriage and Remarriage: To His Wife, Exhortation to Chastity, Monogamy*, Ancient Christian Writers 13 (New York: The Newman Press, 1951), 39.
[44] Le Saint, Introduction, 39.
[45] Le Saint, Introduction, 40.

here is noticeably more negative than that of either *Ad Uxorem* or *Adversus Marcionem*.[46]

Towards the beginning of the work, Tertullian introduced a discussion of God's will and permission as regards marriage and sex. He wrote:

> Now we all recognize God's will when it is clearly manifest, but we ought to understand precisely how it is His will when He makes it known to us. For although it seems that certain things are according to the will of God, since he allows them, yet it does not immediately follow that every permission represents the simple and absolute choice of the one who grants it. A permission is never granted except in a spirit of indulgence.[47]

He brought up this discussion of what could be called God's permissive will in order to highlight the possibility that God might permit things that he did not prefer. He then went on to argue that, in a situation where a person has a choice between something God prefers and something he merely permits, choosing the permitted thing is sinful.[48] If someone chooses permitted things over the things God prefers, Tertullian argued, that person "will be guilty of a kind of disobedience."[49] "When you do what he merely wills and despise what he preferentially wills," he continues, "your choice is more offensive than meritorious. You are, in part, guilty of sin."[50]

After concluding that the one who chooses against God's preference has sinned, Tertullian then applied his thinking to the issue of marriage. Even if God allowed second marriage, Tertullian argued, it is quite clear that he preferred the practice of celibacy and continence.[51] Given that statement of preference, marriage is a questionable choice. As Hunter summarizes, "Since God, through the apostle Paul, had stated his preference for celibacy, failure to follow God's preferential will actually is a kind

---

[46] Le Saint, Introduction, 41.
[47] Tertullian, *Exhortatione Castitatis*, 3, trans. William P. Le Saint, in *Treatises on Marriage and Remarriage: To His Wife, Exhortation to Chastity, Monogamy*, Ancient Christian Writers 13 (New York: The Newman Press, 1951).
[48] Tertullian, *Exhortatione Castitatis*, 3.
[49] Tertullian, *Exhortatione Castitatis*, 3.
[50] Tertullian, *Exhortatione Castitatis*, 3.
[51] Tertullian, *Exhortatione Castitatis*, 3.

of sin" making marriage itself in some way sinful.[52] Second marriage, and even marriage in general, was only according to God's "indulgence," for Tertullian, not "purely and simply according to His will."[53]

Tertullian then went on to examine the passage in 1 Corinthians 7, where Paul gave permission for marriage, saying "it is better to marry than to burn."[54] He argued first that Paul gave his permission, speaking "according to a human way of looking at things, and is not repeating a precept which he has from God."[55] He then continued to argue that the passage was meant to apply only to those who are single or widows when converted and that it should not be used to justify all marriages whatsoever.[56] He also argued that this statement should not be used to argue that marriage is a good at all. He wrote,

> I should like to make clear what sort of "good" that is which is suggested as better than the pain of a punishment, a "good" which cannot be viewed as such except when it is compared with the greatest of all evils, so that only in this relative sense is it good to marry—because it is worse to burn! ... [I]f we are obliged to all it "good" by comparison with something that is evil, then it is not so much a good as it is a kind of lesser evil.[57]

Tertullian interpreted the "burn" of 1 Corinthians 7:9 as referring to burning in hell, rather than burning with passion, as some modern translations do, and on that basis he suggested that it was wrong to use this verse to argue that marriage is good. If marriage is only good in comparison to burning in hell, then it is not truly good, and does not deserve to be treated as such. At very least, he argued, this passage should not be used as conclusive evidence that marriage is good.[58] Though the precise implications of Tertullian's view of marriage are not spelled out here, it is clear that he did not approve of the use of Paul to justify second marriages, and he believed

---

[52] Hunter, *Marriage*, 117.
[53] Tertullian, *Exhortatione Castitatis*, 3.
[54] Tertullian, *Exhortatione Castitatis*, 3, quoting 1 Corinthians 7:9.
[55] Tertullian, *Exhortatione Castitatis*, 3.
[56] Tertullian, *Exhortatione Castitatis*, 3.
[57] Tertullian, *Exhortatione Castitatis*, 3.
[58] Tertullian, *Exhortatione Castitatis*, 3.

that it was far superior, and far more in accordance with the will of God, to remain celibate.

A few sections later in the treatise, Tertullian addressed the issue of sexual intercourse directly. In the course of a discussion of the polygamy practiced by the patriarchs, he examined the command in Genesis to "increase and multiply" and its bearing on marriage. He argued that the command is no longer in force for the Christian because it had been "superseded by the warning that the time is short and that it remaineth that they also who have wives act as if they had none."[59] In saying that those who have wives should act as if they had not, Tertullian argued, God has "abolished" the command to propagate the human race from Genesis 2.[60] Marriage and sex, or at least the multiple marriages of the patriarchs, which God at one time allowed in order to increase the population, are no longer allowed because God has rescinded his permission.[61] Tertullian was not clear about the precise extent to which God's permission to marry and produce offspring has been removed, but he was certain that the permission was always an "indulgence" and that the list of things permitted by God relative to marriage and sex have changed.[62]

Likely the most significant passage for Tertullian's view of sexual desire and sexual intimacy within marriage in *Exhortatione Castitatis* comes about halfway through the treatise, where he made the statement that "second marriage is really nothing but a kind of fornication."[63] He supported this argument by quoting Jesus' statement in Matthew 5:28 that the person who looks at a woman to lust after her has committed fornication with her in his heart.[64] From this command, he argued that a person who marries a woman would not have done so, had he not already lusted after her, and so committed fornication.[65] Further, he noted that the action of looking with lust is the same whether the person is married or unmarried,

---

[59] Tertullian, *Exhortatione Castitatis*, 6.
[60] Tertullian, *Exhortatione Castitatis*, 6.
[61] Tertullian, *Exhortatione Castitatis*, 6.
[62] Tertullian, *Exhortatione Castitatis*, 6.
[63] Tertullian, *Exhortatione Castitatis*, 9.
[64] Tertullian, *Exhortatione Castitatis*, 9.
[65] Tertullian, *Exhortatione Castitatis*, 9.

and therefore concluded that "marriage and fornication are different only because laws appear to make them so."[66] He went on:

> [Marriage and fornication] are not intrinsically different, but only in the degree of their illegitimacy. For what is it that all men and women do in both marriage and fornication? They have sexual relations, of course; and the very desire to do this, our Lord says, is the same thing as fornication.[67]

Lest there be any question about whether Tertullian meant his statement to apply to second marriages only, he clarified, "But then, it is objected, is not your doctrine destructive of all marriage, even monogamy? — Yes, and with good reason, since this, too, in the shameful act which constitutes its essence, is the same as fornication."[68] Given this passage, Hunter commented that, in Tertullian's view, "marriage actually is a sin, that is, a kind of fornication (*stuprum*)."[69] For Tertullian, the command of Jesus in Matthew 5:28 means that all sexual desire or action is wrong or shameful, regardless of the context of that action or desire.

Tertullian did give some allowance for a first marriage later in his argument, but even this is portrayed very negatively. He wrote, "Be grateful if God has been so indulgent as to permit you to marry once. ... Is it not enough that you have slipped from the level of immaculate virginity to the level next beneath is by getting married?"[70] Here he portrayed even a first marriage as allowed but only with begrudging permission, and it is undoubtedly inferior to lifelong celibacy.[71] He also suggested that because even a first marriage was an incidence of incontinence, a second marriage was a significant step towards further and far worse incontinence.[72]

From this discussion of inferiority of marriage to celibacy, Tertullian then went on to praise the benefits of celibacy, speaking in a very negative way about the impacts of sexual intimacy on spirituality. He commented,

---

[66] Tertullian, *Exhortatione Castitatis*, 9.
[67] Tertullian, *Exhortatione Castitatis*, 9.
[68] Tertullian, *Exhortatione Castitatis*, 9.
[69] Hunter, *Marriage*, 118.
[70] Tertullian, *Exhortatione Castitatis*, 9.
[71] Tertullian, *Exhortatione Castitatis*, 9.
[72] Tertullian, *Exhortatione Castitatis*, 9.

speaking of his own experience, "How much better a man feels when he happens to be away from his wife. He has a fine appreciation of spiritual things."[73] He then mentioned such "spiritual things" as closeness to heaven, focus on Scripture, joyful singing, and confident exorcism as benefits of being separated from one's spouse in statements that stand in stark contrast to his high praise of Christian marriage from the final section of his earlier letter to his wife.[74] Further, from Paul's suggestion in 1 Corinthians 7:5 that spouses might mutually agree to abstinence for the purpose of prayer, Tertullian concluded that the apostle really believed that total abstinence is the most beneficial for prayer. He wrote,

> He [the Apostle Paul] wishes us to realize that a policy which is temporarily expedient out to be made permanent, so that it may be permanently expedient. Men need prayer every day and every moment of the day; and if prayer was necessary, so, also was continence.[75]

He also made mention of the force of shame in preventing prayer.[76] Though he did not explain where the shame that prevents prayer came from, the context would suggest that he believed there was a degree of shame involved in sexual intercourse even within the context of marriage. Finally, he concluded that marriage and sexual intimacy dull one's spirituality and suppress the Holy Spirit.[77] From these statements, it is very clear that Tertullian saw marriage and sex as a hindrance rather than a help to piety and spiritual growth, and for this reason he recommended that they be avoided, or at least not entered into a second time.

De Anima

Tertullian's *De Anima* or *On the Soul* is one of his more well-known works. In it, he sought to craft a response to the pagan philosophical positions on the soul that were prevalent in his day, providing a uniquely Christian perspective on psychology.[78] The work shows significant influence from

---

[73] Tertullian, *Exhortatione Castitatis*, 10.
[74] Tertullian, *Exhortatione Castitatis*, 10.
[75] Tertullian, *Exhortatione Castitatis*, 10.
[76] Tertullian, *Exhortatione Castitatis*, 10.
[77] Tertullian, *Exhortatione Castitatis*, 11.
[78] Edwin Quain, Introduction to *On the Soul*, in *Tertullian: Apologetical Works and Minucius*

Tertullian's Writings

Montanist ideas, particularly in one section on dreams, which Tertullian believed could be a means of revelation.[79] Since there is evidence of Montanist influence, but not of any breaking of communion with others, *De Anima* is typically dated to sometime before between 206 and 212, with some placing it after 208 and others arguing for a slightly earlier date.[80]

Though most of *De Anima* does not focus on sexual intercourse, it does include one section that contains some of Tertullian's most explicit writing on the subject. The section comes in the course of Tertullian's discussion of the origin of the soul. In contrast to Platonic ideas of an eternal soul that is transferred into the body in the womb, Tertullian argued that body and soul come into being at the same time and by the same method.[81] He wrote, "Even though we admit that there are two kinds of seed, the one for the body and the other for the soul, we still insist that they are unseparated and as such altogether contemporaneous in origin."[82] He clearly affirmed that life begins at conception and then defended that by discussing his perspective on the sexual act itself.[83] He wrote,

> Nature should, for us, be an object of reverence and not the occasion of blushes. It is lust that had befouled the intercourse of the sexes, not the natural use of this function. It is the excess and not the normal activity which is unclean. Thus has natural intercourse been blessed by God: "Increase and multiply."[84]

From this, it seems that Tertullian saw an appropriate place for sex, but what that place was is not clear.

Following his statement about the place of sex, Tertullian also spoke to the nature of the sexual act itself, calling it an act of both soul and body. He wrote,

---

Felix: Octavius, Fathers of the Church 10 (New York: Fathers of the Church, 1950), 165–166.

[79] Quain, Introduction to "On the Soul," 168.

[80] Roger Pearse ("A Possible Chronology," *The Tertullian Project*, last modified February 18, 2000. http://www.tertullian.org/chronology.htm) dates the treatise between 208–212, while Erik Osborn (*Tertullian: First Theologian of the West*, 10) suggests it may have been written earlier.

[81] Quain, Introduction to *On the Soul*, 167.

[82] Tertullian, *De Anima* 27.4, trans. Edwin A. Quain, in *Tertullian: Apologetical Works and Minucius Felix: Octavius*, Fathers of the Church 10 (New York: Fathers of the Church, 1950).

[83] Tertullian, *De Anima* 27.3–4.

[84] Tertullian, *De Anima* 27.4.

> The soul supplies the desire and the body its gratification; the soul furnishes the impulse, the body affords its realization. By the united impulse of both substances, the whole man is stirred and the seminal substance discharged is a products [sic] of both; the body supplying the fluidity, the soul, warmth.[85]

He went on even to suggest that there is a spiritual component even to orgasm itself, writing, "Is it not a fact that in the moment of orgasm, when the generative fluid is ejected, do we not feel that we have parted with a portion of our soul? As a result, do we not feel weak and faint, along with the blurring of our sight? This, then, must be the seed of the soul."[86] Tertullian did not discuss the implications of this view of the sexual act, but his view does parallel the common cultural understanding of sex in the wider culture, including the celebrated doctor Galen, who advocated abstention from sex on the basis of the loss of soul/warmth involved in sexual intimacy.[87] Whether Tertullian read Galen is unclear, but it does seem likely that his views were at least influenced by the same cultural perspective.

Tertullian did briefly reference sexual desire again in his discussion of the puberty of the soul, though again his views are not entirely clear. He argued that just as the body goes through a time of puberty, so also the soul experiences puberty as it reaches maturity and sexual desire is awakened.[88] At this time, also, a person first experiences shame.[89] He spoke of the puberty of the soul in very similar language to the biblical description of the fall, saying,

> From this age when the genitals cause blushing and must be covered, concupiscence is fostered by the eyes, which in turn communicate desire to the mind, until a full knowledge has been attained. Then man covers himself with fig leaves which themselves excite passion and is driven out of the paradise of his innocence. From there he falls into unnatural vices, which are the perversion of nature's laws.[90]

---

[85] Tertullian, *De Anima* 27.5.
[86] Tertullian, *De Anima* 27.6.
[87] Rouselle, *Porneia*, 14.
[88] Tertullian, *De Anima* 38.1.
[89] Tertullian, *De Anima* 38.2.
[90] Tertullain, *De Anima* 38.2.

While it is not entirely clear what Tertullian was intending to convey here, it does seem that he associated sexual maturity with additional shame and temptation, which would suggest at least a somewhat negative view of sexual desire.

De Monogamia

Tertullian's work *On Monogamy* or *De Monogamia* is his most polemical on the subject of marriage and sexuality. Many of his arguments are similar to those of his earlier work, *Exhortatione Castitatis*, but he took his conclusions even further, not only arguing that it is better not to marry a second time, but that it is sinful. He actively distinguished between those who shared his understanding that second marriages are wrong and those who he deemed "sensualists" who allow second marriages.[91] It is this distinction, according to some scholars, that marks Tertullian's complete conversion to Montanism.[92] Tertullian's views had been pronounced heretical by some, and it is to them that the treatise is primarily addressed.[93] Because of the clear separation drawn between those who hold to Montanist views and others who do not, the treatise is dated between 212 and 222.[94] The treatise claims to have been written one hundred and sixty years after the writing of 1 Corinthians.[95] If this is assertion its accurate, the treatise would be likely be dated to around 217, assuming the conventional date of 57 B.C.E. for the writing of 1 Corinthians.[96] Given the challenges of dating the epistles, along with the uncertainly of Tertullian's claim, this date is far from certain, though connections between Tertullian's other works would support a date of around 217 or before.[97]

As mentioned above, many of Tertullian's points in *De Monogamia* are quite similar to those made in his *Exhortatio Castitatis*, in many cases,

---

[91] Willliam P. Le Saint, Introduction to "Monogamy," by Tertullian, in *Treatises on Marriage and Remarriage: To His Wife, Exhortation to Chastity, Monogamy*, Ancient Christian Writers 13 (New York: The Newman Press, 1951), 67.
[92] Le Saint, Introduction to "Monogamy," 67.
[93] Le Saint, Introduction to "Monogamy," 67.
[94] Le Saint, Introduction to "Monogamy," 68.
[95] Tertullian, *De Monogamia* 3.
[96] Le Saint, Introduction to "Monogamy," 68.
[97] Le Saint, Introduction to "Monogamy," 68.

however, his arguments are strengthened and made even more polemical and negative than in the previous work. For example, at the beginning of the primary section referencing the role of sex in marriage, Tertullian stated that "even if the Paraclete had in our day required complete and absolute virginity or continence, so that the hot passion of lust would not have been permitted gratification in even monogamous marriage, not even such legislation could be considered an innovation."[98] Aside from his Montanist-leaning reference to new revelation, this assertion is significant in how it reveals clearly what is hinted at earlier—that he saw marriage as questionable, if not actually wrong. It is almost as if he was confused at why any marriage was allowed.

Tertullian elucidated this point by arguing along similar lines to his argument in *Exhortatione Castitatis* that the allowance for marriage had been "partially abrogated" by the statement that continence was better. He wrote that because the New Testament affirms that "It is good ... for a man not to touch a woman. Therefore, it is bad to touch one."[99] He continued, "Accordingly, he says that it remaineth that they also who have wives be as if they had none. How much more then does it follow that they who do not have them must not have them!"[100] He suggested, similarly to his argument in *Exhortatione Castitatis*, that "what is merely permitted is not an absolute good."[101] To back up this assertion, he pointed, as in his earlier work, to Paul's statement that "it is better to marry than to burn" (1 Cor. 7:9). This time, however, rather than simply affirming that marriage is only a relative and not a true good, he called it a lesser evil, arguing that "if we are obliged to call it good when it is placed side by side with something evil, then it is not so much a good as it is a lesser evil."[102] He compared marriage with losing an eye, arguing that, though it is better to lose only one eyes than both, both are ultimately evil.[103] Here not only did

---

[98] Tertullian, *De Monogamia* 3.
[99] Tertullian, *De Monogamia* 3, referencing 1 Corinthians 7:1.
[100] Tertullian, *De Monogamia* 3.
[101] Tertullian, *De Monogamia* 3.
[102] Tertullian, *De Monogamia* 3.
[103] Tertullian, *De Monogamia* 3.

he strip marriage of its status as a good, but suggested that it might actually be an evil.[104]

At the end of the section, he did maintain that God had kept intact the allowance for marriage due to the weakness of men, but he portrayed this as almost given grudgingly. He wrote,

> He could have forbidden marriage altogether, and all the more credible that He should have restricted a concession which it would have been perfectly proper to withdraw completely. Here also you ought to recognize the Paraclete as your advocate, since He pleads your weakness as a reason which excuses you from total continence.[105]

Marriage is allowed for believers, but it is only because of the weakness of sinful humanity.

Later in the treatise, Tertullian took up the issue of the command to "increase and multiply," suggesting that the command was no longer in force. He wrote, "But now that the last days which are upon us have abrogated the precept, increase and multiply, the Apostle introduces a new precept: It remaineth that they who have wives be as if they had none, for the time is short."[106] Here, as in a parallel passage in his *Exhortatione Castitatis*, he argued that the original command for mankind to be fruitful has been replaced by the need for total devotion to God, such that even those who are married should live as if they were not.[107] Because the context of this statement refers to the differences between Old Testament morality, as in the command for a brother to marry his brother's widow, it is difficult to tell how this applies to a first marriage, but it is clear that Tertullian did not see the command in Genesis as continuing to hold force for the Christian, as so it could not be used in defense of marriage or sexual activity within marriage.

---

[104] Tertullian, *De Monogamia* 3.
[105] Tertullian, *De Monogamia* 3.
[106] Tertullian, *De Monogamia* 7.
[107] See discussion of Tertullian, *Exhortatione Castitatis* 3 above.

Assessment

Tertullian's writings on marriage and sexuality contain significant tensions which make the construction of a cohesive summary of his perspective quite difficult. From his several works against second marriage, along with *De Cultu Feminarum*, it is clear that he saw sexual activity as potentially problematic even within the bounds of marriage. Conversely, his discussions of marriage in *Adversus Marcionem* and *De Anima* seem to indicate that he did see some legitimacy for the use of sex in marriage, at least when it came to procreation. What is difficult to tell, however, is where he believed the line fell between fornication and the legitimate use of sex within marriage. He seems to have believed that procreation was an appropriate use of sex when done within marriage, based on the command of Genesis 2 to increase and multiply, but he did not see that command as sufficient reason to justify the marriage of believers in the New Testament era. He also spoke quite negatively of sexual desire and, at times, of marriage in general. This appears primarily to have been the result of his concerns about lust, and his belief that even a married person could lust after their spouse, and his concerns about the negative effects that marriage could have on the spiritual life.

3
Tensions & Possible Solutions

Though Tertullian's corpus does not contain any single work that specifically addresses the sexual aspect of the marriage relationship, the topic is touched on in many of his works across his career. The examination of these texts reveals a contrast between his avid defense of marriage and and his slighting of marriage and marital intimacy, once even referring to intimacy as little different form fornication. In multiple cases across his corpus, including *Adversus Marcionem* and *Ad Uxorem*, he spoke glowingly of and ardently defended marriage and married sex, affirming that both were created by God and that it was good for the individual Christian. In other cases, beginning in *De Cultu Feminarum*, and extending through *Exhortation Castitatis* and *De Monogamia*, he spoke very negatively of sexual desire and sexuality, insisting that a Christian woman had no need to dress nicely for her husband and that a life of celibacy was more beneficial for prayer. This tension poses a challenge in determining the precise boundaries of Tertullian's view and an even greater challenge in determining the roots of his ideas.

Montanism and the Old Testament

The tension in Tertullian's thought, between his defense of marriage and unabashed discussion of sexual activity in *Adversus Marcionem* and *De Anima* and his portrayal of marriage as less preferred or even equivalent to fornication in his various works advising against second marriage was also noted by David Hunter in his work *Marriage, Celibacy, and Heresy in Ancient Christianity*.[1] Hunter observed that Tertullian avidly defended both marriage and procreative sex in his argument against Marcion, and pointed out that in *De Anima*, Tertullian talked in detail about the sexual act and affirmed it as "the natural means of propagating the human race that had been decreed by God at the beginning of creation."[2] Hunter also noted the seemingly stark contrast between these descriptions and Tertullian's assertions that marriage was only better when compared with burning in *Ad Uxorum* and that even first marriage was a form of fornication in

---

[1] Hunter, *Marriage*, 116.
[2] Hunter, *Marriage*, 116.

Exhortatione Castitatis.[3] Hunter also pointed to additional evidence of "hostility to sex and marriage" in Tertullian's work on purity.[4]

Hunter's explanation of this tension was two-fold. First, he suggested that Tertullian's negative view of marriage was strongly influenced through his involvement with Montanism. Several of the Montanist priestesses made connections between marriage and sexual activity, and an inability to receive the revelations of the Holy Spirit, seeing sexual renunciation as an element of the eschatological new age that had come in Christ.[5] In support of this explanation, Hunter pointed out that Tertullian quoted one of these Montanist prophetesses in his discussion of the benefits of celibacy in *Exhortatione Castitatis*.[6] Hunter also suggested that the tension in Tertullian's view was related to his distinction between the morality of the Old and New Testaments.[7] According to Hunter, Tertullian saw the encouragement of marriage as relating primarily to the Old Testament era, whereas in the New Testament era, the command to increase and multiply had been "abrogated" by the exhortation of Paul that husbands should live as if they had no wives.[8] Where marriage had been the way of life under the Old Testament, celibacy was now to be the norm in this new era.[9]

Gender, Stoicism, and Eschatology

In her article on Tertullian's view on monogamy, Carly Daniels-Hughes also addressed the tension between Tertullian's works between his honoring of virginity and his support of monogamous marriage.[10] For Daniels-Hughes, however, the significant question was not why Tertullian spoke negatively about sex within the context of marriage, but rather why he so

---

[3] Hunter, *Marriage*, 117.
[4] Hunter, *Marriage*, 119.
[5] Hunter, *Marriage*, 117.
[6] Hunter, *Marriage*, 117; Tertullian, *Exhortatione Castitatis* 3.
[7] Hunter, *Marriage*, 118.
[8] Hunter, *Marriage*, 118.
[9] Hunter, *Marriage*, 120.
[10] Carly Daniels-Hughes, "'We Are Called to Monogamy': Marriage, Virginity, and the Resurrection of the Flesh in Tertullian of Carthage," in *Coming Back to Life: The Permeability of Past and Present, Moratality and Immortality, Death and Life in the Ancient Mediterranean*, ed. Frederick S. Tappenden and Carly Daniels-Hughes (Montreal, QC: McGill University Library, 2017), 248-249.

strongly supported monogamous marriage.[11] She pointed out that, though Tertullian did speak honorably of virginity as a means of imitating Christ, he also, in several of his works against second marriage, spoke of monogamous marriage as founded in the creation order and continuing into eternity.[12] Though he clearly stated that the genitals would no longer serve a sexual function in the resurrection, he also in several places indicated his belief that the bond of marriage exists even after death, suggesting that marriage itself would continue in the resurrection.[13]

Daniels-Hughes argued that Tertullian may have placed emphasis on monogamy for several reasons. First, life without a spouse would have seemed very difficult for men and women in his culture, as men depended on women to run their homes and both sexes felt a deep need to produce children.[14] Because of this, she suggested, Tertullian might have felt the need to make a greater allowance for marriage than his preference for complete chastity would suggest.[15]

Daniels-Hughes also suggested that Tertullian held a view of the connection between body and soul that was similar to the Stoics, which led him to see gender, including a male-over-female hierarchy, as necessarily reflected in the soul as well as the body.[16] This belief, she argued, caused virginity to be "unsettling" for Tertullian, because in renouncing sex, women in some ways renounced gender as well.[17] By promoting eternal monogamy, rather than virginity, as the ideal and by connecting femininity with the flesh and therefore with shame, Daniels-Hughes suggested, Tertullian was able to side-step the issue of gender renunciation and maintain a hierarchy of male and female in the resurrection.[18] Marriage also, she maintained provided an arena in which Tertullian could encourage sexual restraint while retaining the traditional gender roles.[19]

---

[11] Daniels-Hughes, "We Are Called to Monogamy," 248–249.
[12] Daniels-Hughes, "We Are Called to Monogamy," 249–250.
[13] Daniels-Hughes, "We Are Called to Monogamy," 246, 251.
[14] Daniels-Hughes, "We Are Called to Monogamy," 252.
[15] Daniels-Hughes, "We Are Called to Monogamy," 252.
[16] Daniels-Hughes, "We Are Called to Monogamy," 252–253.
[17] Daniels-Hughes, "We Are Called to Monogamy," 253.
[18] Daniels-Hughes, "We Are Called to Monogamy," 260–261.
[19] Daniels-Hughes, "We Are Called to Monogamy," 261.

Assessment

Both Daniels-Hughes and Hunter's answers to the problem contain a measure of helpful insight. If true, Hunter's suggested connection with Montanist ideas would give a degree of clarity to the source of Tertullian's discomfort with marriage and married sex. His connection with Tertullian's perspective on the Old Testament as superseded could likewise be helpful, though it fails to take account of the fact that Tertullian used the authority of Old Testament to justify marriage even in his own day in his work against Marcion. Daniel-Hughes' argument that Tertullian may have been less vehement against marriage due to the cultural belief of the necessity of marriage is insightful, especially because he does mention pressure towards marriage, though the fact he explicitly rejects the two motivations she mentions in his works is cause for question.[20] Her suggestion that Tertullian honored monogamy over virginity as a means of maintaining the hierarchy between men and women in the resurrection is perhaps the most dubious of the claims advanced by either author. Though he did root monogamy and hierarchy in creation, nowhere in his works on marriage did he directly connect marriage with the hierarchy, and his justification for even first marriage tended to be in the command for the production of children, which Daniels-Hughes never addressed. A common thread between both Hunter and Daniels-Hughes, however, was the suggestion of cultural influence on Tertullian's ideas, connecting the tension in Tertullian's ideas with Montanism, wider cultural pressure, and Stoic metaphysics. It is to this potential solution that we will now turn.

Possible Influences

A striking similarity between the views of Hunter and Daniels-Hughes about the tension in Tertullian's views of sexuality is their connection of his views to significant influences in his life. Though they primarily identified Montanism and Stoicism as potential influences, a detailed study not only strengthens the argument for influence in those areas, but also suggests similarities and connections between Tertullian's view of sex and several other sources that have been thought to have influenced his views in other areas, including medical researchers such as Soranus and Galen,

---

[20] Tertullian, *Exhortatione Castitatis* 12; *Ad Uxorum* 1.5.

and wider cultural values for purity. Interestingly, with the exception of Montanism, the potential sources of influence Tertullian's views almost exactly parallel the areas in which there was a high value for sexual purity or a significant movement towards sexual restraint in the first three centuries of the common era.

Soranus and Galen

The way Tertullian spoke about sex in *De Anima* has significant parallels to those of the dominant medical thinkers of his day, who also were ambivalent about the value of sex. He seems to have held to their belief that part of the soul is lost through the ejaculation of semen in orgasm. Though he did not directly connect this with his views on sexual desire, his partial rejection of sex seems consistent with their thought. This connection is especially interesting because there is convincing evidence that Tertullian was familiar with the works of at least two of these thinkers, Soranus and Galen, which makes their influence on him all the more likely.

In chapter 6 of *De Anima*, Tertullian made explicit reference to the gynecological work of Soranus, writing, "[W]e are told by Soranus, a learned medical authority, that material food also benefits the soul. ... This same Soranus has written exhaustive commentary on the soul and he has examined all the theories of the philosophers, too, though in the process of establishing the corporeality of the soul he has robbed it of its immortality."[21] Tertullian also briefly referenced him again in the course of his argument that life begins at conception in chapter 25.[22] While Tertullian did not explicitly reference Soranus in his discussion the issue of sex in relation to the creation of the soul, significant parallels between the view espoused by Tertullian and that of Soranus were noted by Robert Brennan in his assessment of Tertullian's use of science and by Thomas Heyne in his work on Tertullian and obstetrics.[23] Heyne also commented that Tertullian "had a

---

[21] Tertullian, *De Anima* 6.6.
[22] Tertullian, *De Anima* 25.
[23] Robert Brennan, "Re-examining Tertullian and Augustine's Relationship for the Theology Science Dialogue," *Science & Christian Belief* 27, no. 1 (2015): 98, n70; Thomas Heyne, "Tertullian and Obstetrics," in *Studia Patristica, Volume LXV: Papers Presented at the Sixteenth International Conference on Patristic Studies held in Oxford 2011, Volume 13: The First Two Centuries, Apocrypha Tertullian and Rhetoric, From Tertullian to Tyconius*, ed. Markus Vinzent (Leuven:Peeters, 2013), 420.

remarkably positive view of medicine" in general.[24] Given this evidence, it seems likely that Tertullian would have been familiar with Soranus' stance on the dangers of sex and the health benefits of abstinence, which may have in turn influenced his perspectives on its use in the context of marriage.

Another significant figure in the medical literature of Rome who advocated for sexual abstinence was Galen. Though Tertullian never made explicit reference to Galen, Petr Kitzler has argued that Tertullian may have been familiar with his work as well as that of Soranus.[25] In Tertullian's work on the incarnation, *De Carne Christi*, he discussed the normal way in which children are conceived, which he believed resulted from the union of sperm and menstrual fluid.[26] This reference is remarkable because the view it depicts was not the view held by Soranus, who is thought to be Tertullian's chief source of medical knowledge.[27] Though a somewhat similar view was held by Aristotle, Tertullian's depiction bears stronger resemblance to Galen's view, including the use of very similar language for the changes that result from the union of sperm and menses.[28] Kitzler suggested that these similarities are evidence that Tertullian may have been aware of the work of Galen, as well as that of Soranus, despite the assertion of Thomas Heyne to the contrary.[29]

Stoicism

In addition to evidence of connections with medical sources, there also seems to have been a relationship between Tertullian's views and those of Stoic philosophers. Though Tertullian is famous for his statement condemning the joining of Athens and Jerusalem in a mixture of Christianity with Greek philosophy, some have argued that he himself was deeply influenced by Stoic philosophy in a variety of areas, including that of ethics.[30] Eric Osborn, who also wrote a prominent biography of Tertullian, noted a

---

[24] Heyne, "Tertullian and Obstetrics," 428.
[25] Petr Kitzler, "Tertullian and Ancient Embryology in *De carne Christi* 4, 1 and 19, 3-4," *Zeitschrift für antikes Christentum* 18, no. 2 (2014): 204-209.
[26] Kitzler, "Tertullian and Ancient Embryology," 205.
[27] Kitzler, "Tertullian and Ancient Embryology," 205.
[28] Kitzler, "Tertullian and Ancient Embryology," 207-208
[29] Kitzler, "Tertullian and Ancient Embryology," 209; Heyne, "Tertullian and Obstetrics," 421.
[30] Eric Osborn, "Christianity and Classical Thought," *Studia Missionalia* 44 (1995): 79.

Tensions & Possible Solutions

wide variety of areas in which he believed Tertullian was influenced by Stoicism, including his ideas of substance and relations in his doctrine of the trinity and his two-natures Christology.[31] Osborn argued that Tertullian's love of paradox, which is particularly notable in his defense of the incarnation but also may perhaps be seen in the tensions of his views of marriage and celibacy, was itself a common feature of Stoicism.[32] Osborn also pointed to Tertullian's use of the conscience, law, and nature, in his ethical discussions, and even in some his discussions of sexuality in particular, as further influence of Stoicism.[33]

The possibility of the influence of Stoicism in Tertullian's thought is particularly significant because of the similarity between Tertullian's ideas about sex and those of the Stoics. Tertullian's squeamishness about even married sex, while upholding its validity for the procreation of children, bears a particularly strong resemblance to the ideas of the Stoic Musonius Rufus as discussed above. Even if he never read Rufus directly, the ideas would likely have been present in the discussions in which Tertullian was involved. If Tertullian was familiar with and influenced by Stoic ideas in other areas, it is reasonable to conclude that he may have been influenced in his views of sex as well.

Montanism

Though it is challenging to determine the precise perspective of Montanism on marriage and sex, some have suggested that Tertullian may have been influenced by Montanist teachings in his views on sexuality.[34] As noted above, Tertullian shared many sympathies with Montanist teaching, and is even thought by many to have converted to Montanism towards the end of his life. Given that clear connection, the possibility of influence in this area is worthy of investigation as well.

Little evidence is extant on the Montanist views of marriage and sex, but in his *Historia Ecclesia*, Eusebius references Apollonius' work against the Montanists, suggesting that Montanus himself supported the

---

[31] Osborn, "Christianity and Classical Thought," 85, 87–88.
[32] Osborn, "Christianity and Classical Thought," 81–82.
[33] Osborn, "Christianity and Classical Thought," 83.
[34] David G. Hunter, *Marriage, Celibacy, and Heresy in Ancient Christianity: The Jovianist Controversy*, Oxford Early Christian Studies (Oxford: Oxford University Press, 2007), 117.

annulment of marriages and that both Priscilla and Maximilla left their husbands after becoming prophetesses.[35] Though some debate whether the dissolution of marriage was seen as normative for the church as a whole or merely an element of the vocation of prophetess, due to the fact that not all Montanist communities were totally celibate, there is clear evidence than Montanist communities highly valued celibacy.[36] Christine Trevett, author of a major work on Montanism and gender, also suggested, on the basis of Tertullian's arguments about the illegitimacy of digamy, that Montanists also prohibited second marriages.[37]

A clear connection between Tertullian and the Montanists in the area of sexuality in marriage can be seen in *Exhortatione Castitatis*, where, in the course of extolling the benefits of celibacy for the spiritual life, he wrote, "[T]he holy prophetess Prisca ... says, 'continence effects the harmony of the soul, and the pure see visions and, bowing down, hear voices speaking clearly words salutary and secret.'"[38] This quotation from the Montanist prophetess Prisca (also called Priscilla) is only used as additional evidence to support a case otherwise made from Scripture, and it is not clear the precise authority it holds, but it does seem that Tertullian at least saw his views as in line with those of the Montanists on this issue, whether or not his views were directly influenced by their teachings. Trevett argued that Tertullian was drawn to Montanism because of the beliefs he previously held, rather than suggesting he was influenced by their thinking on this issue, given the fact that his negative opinion of remarriage is seen even in treatises that are typically understood to have been written before he became interested in Montanism, such as *Ad Uxorum*, but the precise connection, and indeed the date of the start of Tertullian's involvement with the Montanists, is unclear.[39]

Since Tertullian is almost the sole extant author speaking from a perspective that is sympathetic to Montanist ideas and because of the dearth of witness to Montanism beliefs and practices it is difficult to determine

---

[35] Eusebius, *Historia Ecclesia* 18.2-3, trans. Arthur Cushman McGiffert.
[36] Christine Trevett, *Montanism: Gender, Authority, and the New Prophecy* (Cambridge: Cambridge University Press, 1996), 110.
[37] Trevett, *Montanism*, 114.
[38] Tertullian, *Exhortatione Castitatis* 10.
[39] Trevett, *Montanism*, 112.

Tensions & Possible Solutions

the degree to which Tertullian may have been influenced by Montanist teachings in the area of sexuality, rather than being drawn to them because of their similar beliefs. It is undoubtedly worthy of note, however, that the Montanists seem to have held a similar tension in their views of marriage to that demonstrated by Tertullian, and that Tertullian quoted them with authority on this issue.

Larger Cultural Influences

In addition to the possible influence of writers in medicine, such as Soranus and Galen, of Stoic philosophers, and of Montanist oracles, there is also evidence in Tertullian's writings of the influence of aspects of the larger culture, such as literature and philosophy. In both *Ad Uxorum* and *Exhortatione Castitatis*, he used examples of chastity in the wider society to further illustrate the value of continence for the Christian. In *Ad Uxorum*, he directed his wife to consider the Vestal Virgins and other pagan priestesses, who were committed to continence even in service of the Devil, writing, "A hard thing it is, forsooth, and arduous, that a Christian woman, out of love for God, should practice continence after her husband's death, when pagans use the priestly offices of virgins and wisdoms in the service of their own Satan."[40] In *Exhortatione Castitatis*, he reinforces the importance of monogamy by referencing cultural custom, writing,

> I may add to this exhortation of mine, dear brother, certain examples given us by the pagans themselves. ... Thus, monogamy is so highly prized by the pagans that when a virgin is married according to the law, a woman who has been wedded only once must act as matron of honor.[41]

Following this example, as well as several more, including the Vestal Virgins and other priestesses, he suggested that, "a Christian, then, is all the more guilty if he refuses to embrace a chastity which effects salvation."[42] Tertullian also specifically referenced the commitment shown by the

---

[40] Tertullian, *Ad Uxorum* 6.
[41] Tertullian, *Exhortatione Castitatis* 13.
[42] Tertullian, *Exhortatione Castitatis* 13.

famous literary heroines Dido and Lucretia as illustrations of his point.[43] Though in all of these cases Tertullian elevated the examples of Christian women as more valuable than those of pagan women, it is clear that he was aware of a cultural value of celibacy.[44] His use of these examples also demonstrates a belief that Christians must be at least as self-controlled as their pagan neighbors, which may have influenced his perspective of sex within the context of marriage and indeed of marriage itself.

Tertullian's emphasis on clothing as related to sexual desire and sexual purity may also be related to cultural factors. His connection of dress as a whole and lust/purity suggests a similar view to that espoused in the wider aristocratic culture.[45] The veiling of women, on which he was insistent, was often a part of the portrayals of women who exemplified *pudicitia*.[46] Also, his comments on women's dress, suggesting that married women should only care about pleasing their husbands with their dress, bear a strong resemblance to the words of Seneca noted about, stating that a women should only be dressed up enough to avoid appearing sloppily dressed.[47] This emphasis, too, suggests that Tertullian's views may have been influenced by the perspectives of the wider culture.

Conclusions

As with many other areas of study of Tertullian, his views on marriage and sexuality are something of a conundrum. In some places he defended and supported marriage, while in others he spoke very negatively of it, and especially of the place of sex within it. He wanted to defend the legitimacy of procreation, yet also to warn against the use of procreation as an excuse for marriage, rather than a commitment to celibacy. Sexual intimacy merely for the sake of pleasure, and certainly any kind of dress to attract the admiration of a spouse, Tertullian roundly condemned as unnecessary, and perhaps even sinful. Though he frequently quoted from Scripture, he did not address some passages that would seem to support the use of sex in

---

[43] Tertullian, *Exhortatione Castitatis* 13.
[44] Tertullian, *Exhortatione Castitatis* 13.
[45] Tertullian, *De Cultu Feminarum* 2.1.4.
[46] See Tertullian, *De Virginibus Velandis*, as well as *De Oratione* 20-21: Langlands, *Sexual Morality*, 69-70.
[47] Tertullian, *De Cultu Feminarum* 2.4.1; Seneca, *Controversiae* 2.7.3

marriage for the purpose of intimacy, the most conspicuous among these being 1 Corinthians 7:3–4. The neglect of these verses is particularly striking given the fact that he frequently referenced the surrounding verses, particularly verse 1, in his arguments against marriage. At very least, Tertullian's writings on married sexuality reveal a tension in his thought between a desire to affirm marriage and significant concerns about the legitimacy of sex.

Precisely what led Tertullian to have the views of sex and marriage that he did is difficult to say, but he does seem to have been influenced by many of the same cultural influences that were behind a movement towards sexual restraint in the wider society outside of Christianity. The medical doctors he read were very squeamish about sex, Stoicism taught restraint as a key virtue of a philosopher, those who were committed to preserving their *pudicitia* even in the face of death were honored in literature, and dress was seen as an essential part of the *pudicitia* of women. Also, there may have been a strain of Montanist thought that saw sex as problematic, at least in some sense, for the reception of prophecy, which could have further influenced his views. With these influences playing a significant role in the culture in which Tertullian found himself, it is unsurprising that he began to have questions about the legitimacy of sex, even in the context of marriage.

The primary means of support Tertullian used for his views was Scripture, and the Scriptures he pointed to do evidence some level of tension as regards the benefits of marriage and celibacy. Christians even today wrestle with what do with Paul's statement that "It is good for a man not to touch a woman" (1 Cor. 7:1) and others like it. Given Tertullian's cultural context, however, it seems likely cultural movement towards sexual restraint and prevalent concerns about the health of sex also influenced his interpretations of those Scriptures, producing the high degree of tension that his evident in his writings.

While Tertullian's views on this issue and his possible influences are interesting on their own, they are made more significant by the fact that Tertullian had great influence on the later tradition as well, particularly as the first major Latin theologian. He is explicitly cited by Cyprian and Jerome, and he almost certainly also had an influence on Augustine in a number of areas. Explicit citations of Tertullian on the subject of marriage are relatively rare in early Christian authors because his negative views on second marriage were a significant area in which he parted ways with the majority of the church, but his views on sexuality bear strong similarities to those of many of the early leaders of the church, including the three figures cited above. Even if these figures were not directly influenced by Tertullian himself in their views of sexuality, they almost certainly would have been aware of the same cultural trends by which Tertullian was influenced and may themselves have been influenced by those things in their views on this issue. Based on the results of this study, a wider evaluation of early Christian views on sexuality within marriage with particular attention to influences and sources of authority is needed to determine the degree to which other theologians may have been influenced by Tertullian or the wider culture in this area.

Acknowledgements

This study would not have been possible without the help and support of many professors, mentors, and dialogue partners who have helped to prepare and assist in the development of this study.

First, I am incredibly thankful to Dr. Michael A.G. Haykin for his guidance, encouragement, and support throughout the process of research, writing, and publication. In the midst of any number of other projects, he made time to guide me through the steps of this project and supported my work for publication. Without his wise counsel and mentorship, I would never have embarked on this project in the first place, let alone bringing it to print.

To Chance Faulkner and H&E publishing, thank you for thinking my little project was worthy of publication and working with my technology challenges.

To my mentors at Colorado Christian University, Dr. Megan DeVore and Dr. David Kotter, thank you for supporting me from the very start. Without their encouragement, I would never have taken up the study of Church history or come to study these things. Megan DeVore especially was helpful in providing additional feedback and resources on early Christian sexuality, Tertullian, and Montanism.

To Dr. Richard Niezen, my Bachelor's thesis supervisor, thank you for teaching me to research and write. This project would never have been manageable without the experience I gained from working with you.

To my husband, Schuyler Turrill, thank you for putting up with countless hours of research, writing, and stressing about research and writing. You have been my sounding board and my encourager, and I'm so very thankful for you.

Finally, I am thankful to my Lord and Savior Jesus Christ. If there is anything of merit in this study, it is all a gift of his overflowing grace. To him be the glory.

Timeline of Tertullian's Works

De Cultu Feminarum – 198–206 – Book 1 and Book 2 seem to have been written separately, but both were written after 198 and before Tertullian's interest in Montanism began.[1]

Ad Uxorum – 200–206 – This work appears to have been written before Tertullian became interested in Montanism, but after his conversion.[2] It discourages remarriage after the death of a spouse, but also contains substantial advice for the eventuality of a remarriage.

Adversus Marcionem – 207–208 – This work went through three editions, but the third, which is extant, is believed to have been published between 207-208. The first edition could have been published as early as 198. The book in its extant edition reveals Montanist sympathies but seems to have been written before Tertullian split completely with the catholic faith.[3]

De Exhortatione Castitatis – 204–212 – This work has been variously dated, but certainly was written before 212. In this work, too, Tertullian seems to have had Montanist sympathies, as evidenced by his quotation of the Montanist oracle Priscilla, but he appears to have remained in communion with the catholic party.[4] This work strongly discourages remarriage but does not explicitly condemn it.

---

[1] Rudolph Arbesmann, Emily Joseph Daly, Edwin Quain, Introduction to "The Apparel of Women," by Tertullian, in *Tertullian: Disciplinary, Moral and Ascetical Works*, The Fathers of the Church 40 (New York: The Fathers of the Church, 1959), 115; Eric Osborn, *Tertullian, First Theologian of the West* (Cambridge: Cambridge University Press, 1997), 9.

[2] William Le Saint, Introduction to "To His Wife," by Tertullian, in *Treatises on Marriage and Remarriage: To His Wife, Exhortation to Chastity, Monogamy*, Ancient Christian Writers 13 (New York: The Newman Press, 1951), 8; Osborn, *Tertullian*, 9.

[3] Ernest Evans, Introduction to *Tertullian: Adversus Marcionem*, by Tertullian (Oxford: Clarendon Press, 1972), xviii; Osborn, *Tertullian*, 9.

[4] William Le Saint, Introduction to "Exhortation to Chastity," by Tertullian, in *Treatises on Marriage and Remarriage: To His Wife, Exhortation to Chastity, Monogamy*, Ancient Christian Writers 13 (New York: The Newman Press, 1951), 39. (*Tertullian*, 10)

De Anima - 208-212 - Here, too, Tertullian displays Montanist sympathies, but appears to remain in communion with the catholic party.[5]

De Monogamia - 212-222 - In this work Tertullian openly distances himself from the catholic party, favoring only Montanist ideas.[6] He explicitly denies the validity of second marriage, and he calls those who disagrees with him "carnal" (*psychichos*).

---

[5] Roger Pearse, "A Possible Chronology," *The Tertullian Project*, last modified February 18, 2000. http://www.tertullian.org/chronology.htm. Osborn dates this a bit earlier to the "middle period" between 207-208 (*Tertullian*, 10).

[6] William Le Saint, Introduction to "Monogamy," by Tertullian, in *Treatises on Marriage and Remarriage: To His Wife, Exhortation to Chastity, Monogamy*, Ancient Christian Writers 13 (New York: The Newman Press, 1951), 68. Le Saint suggests the possibility of 217 as a date, given the reference to Paul's letter to the Corinthians being written 160 years earlier, but he also gives the date range. Osborn dates it between 213 and 222 (*Tertullian*, 10).

Bibliography

Primary Sources

Roman

Cicero. *The Republic*. In *The Republic and The Laws*. Translated by Niall Rudd. Oxford: Oxford University Press, 2008.

Livy. *Roman History, Volume 1: Books 1-2*. Translated by B.O. Foster. Loeb Classical Library 114. Cambridge, MA.: Harvard University Press, 1919.

———. *Roman History, Volume 39: Books 38-40*. Translated by J.C. Yardley. Loeb Classical Library 313. Cambridge, MA.: Harvard University Press, 2018.

Lucan. *The Pharsalia*. Translated by Edward Ridley. London: Longmans, Green, and Co., 1896.

Musonius Rufus. *Miscellanies*. Translated by Cora E. Lutz. In *Musonius Rufus: "The Roman Socrates."* Yale Classical Studies 10. New Haven: Yale University Press, 1947.

Seneca. *Declamations, Volume 1: Controversiae, Books 1-6*. Translated by Michael Winterbottom. Loeb Classical Library 463. Cambridge, MA.: Harvard University Press, 1974.

Soranus. *Gynecology*. Translated by Owsei Tempkin. Baltimore: The Johns Hopkins Press, 1956.

Early Christian

Augustine. *The City of God: Against the Pagans*. Translated by R.W. Dyson. Cambridge Classics in the History of Political Thought. Cambridge: Cambridge University Press, 1998.

———. *De haeresibus ad Quodvultdeus*. Translated by L.G. Muller. *Patristic Studies* 90. Washington: Catholic University of America, 1956.

Eusebius. *History of the Church*. Translated by Arthur Cushman McGiffert. In *Nicene and Post-Nicene Fathers*, Second Series, Vol. 1. Edited by Philip Schaff and Henry Wace. Buffalo, NY: Christian Literature

Publishing Co., 1890.

Tertullian

Tertullian. *Adversus Marcionem, Books 1 to 3*. Translated by Ernest Evans. Oxford: The Clarendon Press, 1972.

———. "An Exhortation to Chastity." Translated by William P. Le Saint. In *Treatises on Marriage and Remarriage: To His Wife, Exhortation to Chastity, Monogamy*. Ancient Christian Writers 13. New York: The Newman Press, 1951.

———. "On the Dress of Women." Translated by Rudolph Arbesmann, Emily Joseph Daly, and Edwin Quain. In *Tertullian: Disciplinary, Moral and Ascetical Works*. Fathers of the Church 40. New York: Fathers of the Church, 1959.

———. "On the Soul." Translated by Edwin A Quain. In *Tertullian: Apologetical Works and Minucius Felix: Octavius*. Fathers of the Church 10. New York: Fathers of the Church, 1950.

———. "Monogamy." Translated by William P. Le Saint. In In *Treatises on Marriage and Remarriage: To His Wife, Exhortation to Chastity, Monogamy*. Ancient Christian Writers 13. New York: The Newman Press, 1951.

———. "To His Wife." Translated by William P. Le Saint. In *Treatises on Marriage and Remarriage: To His Wife, Exhortation to Chastity, Monogamy*. Ancient Christian Writers 13. New York: The Newman Press, 1951.

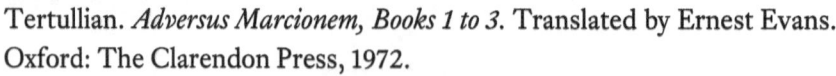

Secondary Sources

Roman Views

Grubbs, Judith Evans. *Law and Family in Late Antiquity: The Emperor Constantine's Marriage Legislation*. Oxford: Clarendon Press, 1995

Langlands, Rebecca. *Sexual Morality in Ancient Rome*. Cambridge: Cambridge University Press, 2006.

Lightman, Marjorie and William Ziesel. "Univira: An Example of Continuity and Change in Roman Society." *Church History* 46, no. 1 (1977): 19–32.

Rousselle, Aline. *Porneia: On Desire and the Body in Antiquity*. Translated by Felicia Pheasant. New York: Barnes and Noble, 1996.

Veyne, Paul. "The Roman Empire." In *A History of Private Life, Volume 1: From Pagan Rome to Byzantium*. Translated by Arthur Goldhammer. Cambridge, MA.: The Belknap Press, 1987.

Tertullian

Daniels-Hughes, Carly. "'We Are Called to Monogamy': Marriage, Virginity, and the Resurrection of the Flesh in Tertullian of Carthage." In *Coming Back to Life: The Permeability of Past and Present, Moratality and Immortality, Death and Life in the Ancient Mediterranean*. Edited by Frederick S. Tappenden and Carly Daniels-Hughes, 239–265. Montreal, QC: McGill University Library, 2017.

Dunn, Geoffrey. *Tertullian*. New York: Routledge, 2004.

Hunter, David G. *Marriage, Celibacy, and Heresy in Ancient Christianity: The Jovianist Controversy*. Oxford Early Christian Studies. Oxford: Oxford University Press, 2007.

Osborn, Eric. *Tertullian, First Theologian of the West*. Cambridge: Cambridge University Press, 1997.

———. "Christianity and Classical Thought." *Studia Missionalia* 44 (1995): 69–90.

Trevett, Christine. *Montanism: Gender, Authority, and the New Prophecy*. Cambridge: Cambridge University Press, 1996

Index

A

Abortion, 21
Abstinence, 16, 17, 20, 30, 36, 48
Adams, Thomas, 2
Adultery, 13, 14, 15, 16, 18, 19, 25
Apollonius, 49
Aquinas, Thomas, 4, 5
Aristotle, 48
Asceticism, 29
Asterius of Amasea, 6, 7
Augustan marriage laws, 16
Augustine, 5, 6, 7, 13, 22, 47, 53, 59
Augustus, 11

B

Baptism, 22, 29
Baxter, Richard, 1, 2, 5
Beauty, 25, 26, 28
Bede, 5, 7
Bullinger, Heinrich, 3

C

Calvin, Idelette, 3
Calvin, John, xi, 3, 4
Cataphrygians. *See* Montanism
Cato, 18
Celibacy, 4, 5, 7, 8, 27, 29, 30, 32, 34, 35, 43, 44, 49, 50, 52, 53
Chastity, 14, 27, 29, 30, 45, 51
Childbirth, 16
Christology, 49
Church fathers, 22
Cicero, 13, 59
Claudia Quinta, 12
Cleaver, Robert, 2
Clement of Alexandria, 7, 8
Conception, 21, 37, 47
Conscience, 49
Constantine, 8, 15, 60
Cult of Bacchus, 15
Cyprian, 53

D

Divorce, 6, 16, 29
Double standards, 19

E

Eusebius, 49, 50, 59

F

Fornication, 22, 25, 27, 28, 34, 35, 42, 43

G

Galen, 17, 38, 46, 47, 48, 51
Gender, 16, 45
Gluttony, 30
Gnosticism, 7, 8
Gouge, William, 2
Greek philosophy, 48

H

Heaven, 36
Holy Spirit, 6, 36, 44
Husbands, 13, 19, 25, 26, 28, 51, 55

I

Ignatius of Antioch, 9

J

Jerome, 5, 53
Justinian, 11
Juvenal, 11, 12

L

Libertinism, 11, 20
Livy, 12, 13, 15, 19, 59
Lucan, 18, 19, 59
Lust, 13, 18, 25, 34, 37, 40, 42, 52

M

Macarius, 6
Marcion, 21, 28, 29, 31, 43, 46
Marriage, 1, 2, 3, 4, 5, 6, 7, 8, 9, 10, 11, 15, 16, 18, 20, 22, 25, 26, 27, 28, 29, 30, 31, 32, 33, 34, 35, 36, 39, 40, 41, 42, 43, 44, 45, 46, 48, 49, 50, 51, 52, 53, 54
Medical, 11, 17, 19, 20, 46, 47, 48, 53
Mixed marriage (between believer and unbeliever), 28
Modesty, 13, 24, 25, 28
Monasticism, 7, 8
Monogamy, 11, 35, 44, 45, 46, 51
Montanism, 22, 23, 24, 26, 29, 31, 37, 39, 40, 43, 44, 46, 49, 50, 51, 53, 55, 57, 58, 61
Montanus, 49

O

Octavian, 15

P

Polygamy, 34
Prayer, xi, 5, 36, 43
Pregnancy, 16

Prisca (Montanist prophetess), 31, 50
Procreation, 5, 6, 7, 18, 20, 30, 31, 42, 49, 52
Propertius, 12
Prostitution, 15, 18, 19
Puberty, 38
Puritans, 1, 2, 3, 5

R

Rape, 14, 19
Reformation, xi, 2, 3, 4
Remarriage, 22, 26, 31, 32, 33, 34, 35, 39, 42, 43, 45, 50, 54, 57, 58
Resurrection, 45, 46
Rousselle, Aline, 17, 18
Rufus, Musonius, 18, 19, 20, 49, 59

S

Satan, 7, 51
Saturninus, 7
Science, 47
Second Lateran Council, 4
Semen, 16, 17, 47, 48
Seneca, 11, 12, 13, 19, 52, 59
Sexual desire, 16, 23, 24, 25, 26, 34, 35, 38, 39, 42, 47, 52
Sexual intimacy, 1, 3, 5, 6, 20, 29, 31, 34, 35, 36, 38
Sexual purity, 11, 12, 47, 52
Slavery, 11, 12, 13, 15, 16, 19
Soranus, 16, 17, 46, 47, 48, 51, 59
Soranus of Ephesus, 16
Soul, 6, 18, 21, 36, 37, 38, 45, 47, 50
Spiritual growth, 36
Stoicism, 44, 45, 46, 48, 49, 53

T

Taylor, Edward, 3
Tertullian
   conversion, 22
   influence of Stoicism, 49
   involvement with Montanism, 22
   lay person, 22
   marriage, 22, 26
Trinitarian theology, 21

V

Viret, Pierre, 3
Virginity, 4, 17, 35, 40, 44, 45, 46

W

Westminster Confession of Faith, 3
Widows, 16, 27, 29, 33, 41
Wives, 12, 13, 22, 25, 26, 27, 28, 31, 36, 51
Women, 2
Women's apparel, 13, 23, 24, 52, 53

Scripture Index

Old Testament

Genesis
    2:23   7
    2:24   9
Proverbs
    5:18–19   2

New Testament

Matthew
    5:28   27, 39, 40
1 Corinthians
    6:16–17   11
    7:1   61
    7:3-4   61
    7:5   41
    7:9   37, 46
    7:13–15   31
1 Timothy
    4:1–4   8